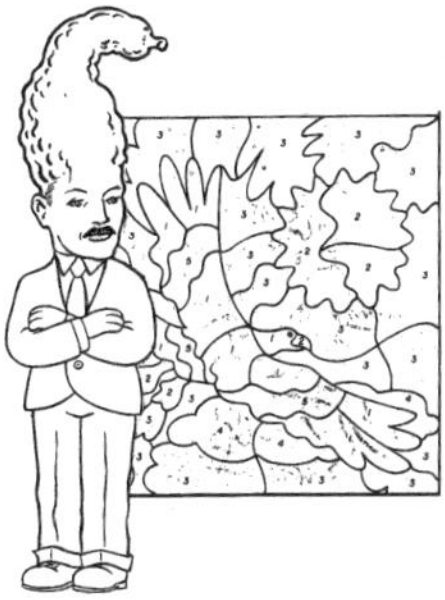

NEW YORK'S
new and avant-garde
art galleries

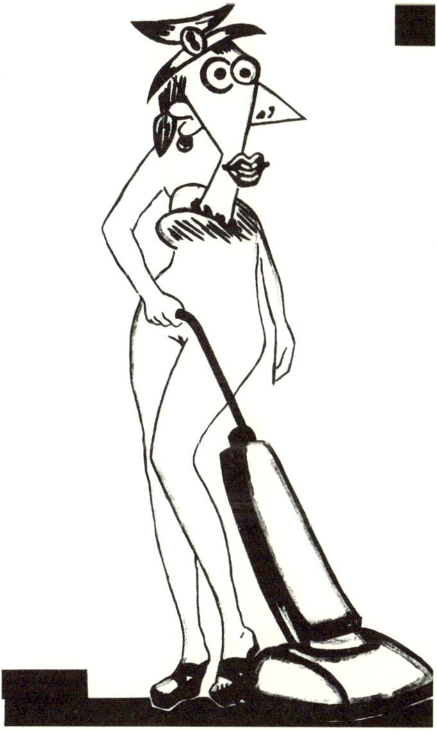

Barbara Stone

Art by
Steve Gianakos

A CITY & COMPANY GUIDE • NEW YORK

Library of Congress Cataloging in Publication Data is available upon request.
ISBN 1-885492-82-0
First Edition
Printed in the United States of America

Special editions of City & Company books can be created to specification.
Contact the Sales Director at:
City & Company 22 West 23rd St. New York, NY 10010

With some galleries in this book planning to move or rumored to be moving, it is advisable to call and confirm location before making a special trip.

PUBLISHER'S NOTE
No fees were paid or services rendered for inclusion in these pages. While every effort was made to ensure accuracy at the time of publication, it is always wise to phone ahead and confirm hours, and artists currently represented.

10 9 8 7 6 5 4 3 2 1

Contents

INTRODUCTION

Of New York City's nearly inexhaustible supply of diversions, few can offer the unrestricted pleasures of visiting art galleries. The most democratic of cultural activities, gallery-going exacts no admission fees, requires no reservations, and won't hold you accountable for stomping out in a huff if you don't like what you see.

Besides the diversity of the art itself—which can range from ordinary and pretty to far-out and ugly, from intellectually engaging to funny and confounding, from traditional to so avant-garde that neither content nor materi-

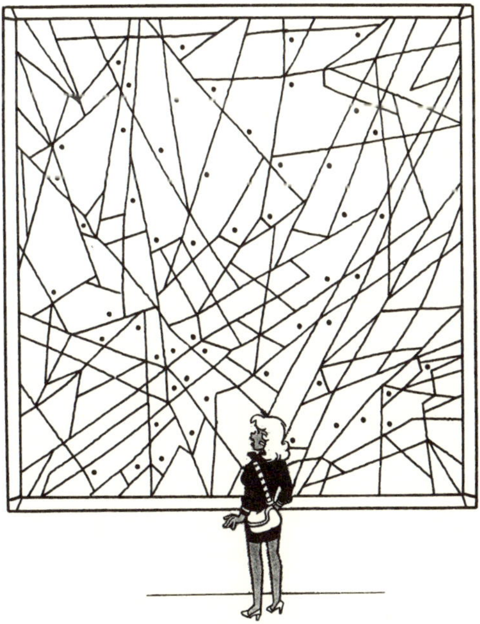

als can be deciphered—is the reality that galleries are often the only places where such art can be seen. Most of the galleries in this compendium specialize in modern and contemporary art, showing generally new art.

Museums, for the most part, show work that has already been validated and then approved by institutional boards and committees. Galleries aren't fettered by such constraints. They offer an up-to-date barometer of the artistic moment—a showplace for the emerging as well as the established artist. And, of course, they sell the art, and in such a wide price range that even the financially challenged novice can indulge.

With some 750 commercial galleries dotting the city—a number that fluctuates daily—in ever-changing locations (some, like Marlborough, PaceWildenstein, Gagosian, and Feigen have a couple of branches, usually one in midtown or on the Upper East Side and another downtown or in Chelsea), the task of seriously distilling the list was arduous and the results in some ways arbitrary. It required drawing rather strict parameters. The galleries chosen are all commercial ones, that is, those that sell art, as opposed to the many not-for-profit spaces that principally exhibit art.

What you'll find here are the ones that are strongest in specific areas. Most of them are well established, in the sense that they have a track record and are likely to remain in business. Some, however, are notable for quickly asserting their presence by revealing a keen eye for important new work. Others have narrow specialty areas, such as photography or works on paper, or focus on a particular region, such as Asia, Africa, or Latin America. They all have identifiable profiles—a style or a sensibility that defines their taste.

New York's many galleries span the length and breadth of the city and even cross bridges into other boroughs. For reasons of space and simplicity, I've limited the selections to Manhattan and, even there, to the most gallery-populated areas: namely, Chelsea, SoHo, TriBeCa, and 57th Street and environs. Be aware, however, that not only are galleries changing spaces in record number, but artists, too, frequently switch their affiliation. For these reasons, the art and artists described in these pages should be taken as samples of the kind of work a gallery favors.

Other guides and listings—especially the *Art Now Gallery Guide*, and *Simon Says* (which you can pick up gratis at the reception desk of many galleries), as well as *New York* magazine, *The New Yorker, Time Out New York,* and *The New York Times* (notably the Friday Weekend section)—can expertly direct you to the many other venues throughout the boroughs, particularly some of the lively new spaces in Brooklyn, Queens, and the Bronx. Two invaluable reference books are *New York Contemporary Art Galleries: The Complete Annual Guide,* by Renée Phillips (Manhattan Arts), and the *Art in America Annual Guide;* both offer comprehensive listings.

With new galleries opening in upper Manhattan, near the George Washington Bridge, and in Harlem, as well as a bunch down near Wall Street and in the East Village and West Village, you'd be best off beginning in the most concentrated areas. Before embarking on a tour, first-time visitors and even veteran traipsers are well advised to plan their itinerary and limit their daily rounds by district. Most galleries are open Tuesday through Saturday, although this may vary and should always be checked in advance. But all the galleries included here do have regular hours, unlike some private dealers, who require appointments, and most have summer hours, often closing on Saturdays in July and the entire month of August. Many also hold exhibition opening receptions, generally in the evenings somewhere between 5 and 8 o'clock, and these are often open to the public. To find out times and locations, your best bet is to check the *Gallery Guide,* which comes out monthly.

The aim of this book is to help the novice as well as the veteran art lover tap into a broad and complicated art network, where information is shared generously and where people—often in outlandish attire—gather to see shows and one another after work and on weekends. It's a constantly changing scene, filled with intellectual stimulation, surprise, fun, and much more. And for those who are interested in buying art, there's a great deal available, and at prices that won't have you hocking your dog or children—unless you want to.

As for the art, Steve Gianakos has enthusiastically captured the spirit of the city's gallery scene today—the fun as well as the edginess. He offers an amused and sometimes satiric look at the characters—artists, dealers, and visitors alike. Only on occasion does he represent the actual art shown at a particular space, since while the spirit of the gallery remains relatively constant, what the artist might create is anyone's guess.

Ace Gallery

275 Hudson Street,
Between Spring and Canal streets
(212) 255-5599
Tuesday through Saturday,
10 A.M. to 6 P.M.

Classic contemporary movements from the 1960s; established and emerging artists from 1980 to the present

For those who expect a gallery to be a sleek, white, rectangular backdrop for the art that fills it, stepping into Ace—that is, if they can find the excessively unprepossessing entrance—may be something of a shock. Instead of providing a stark ground for a bold array of work, the gallery assumes more the posture of a tomb for contemporary pharaohs—or, as the art critic Jerry Saltz puts it, "our Xanadu." Enormous rooms on either side of a cavernous hall, strictly unadorned, offer a neutral, rather gruff showcase for massive installations and large canvases. Gray concrete is the ruling esthetic.

With 25,000 square feet, there's room for all kinds of shenanigans, including shows like that of Tim Hawkinson's ersatz inventions made out of lots of junk. Ace is a perfect fit for the neighborhood. Warehouses still line the far-West streets, just above Canal, where the traffic heads south to the New Jersey-bound Holland Tunnel. Garages and secondhand shops as well as new-furniture showrooms dot the area, and so do chic restaurants, like the much-loved Alison on Dominick.

The works on view at the gallery almost always look as if they were permanent fixtures. Opened in 1994 by Los Angeles transplant Douglas Chrismas, who still maintains his L.A. space, Ace specializes in all the big contemporary movements: Abstract Expressionism, Minimalism, and Conceptualism. Besides Hawkinson's jury-rigged body parts and machines, you might discover Michael Heizer's outsize sculptures perforated with Swiss-cheese holes, looking as if they had been plucked from the excavation of a prehistoric site. Or Jannis Kounellis's gargantuan burlap-and-found-object installations. Kounellis is one of the best known of the artists of the Italian-born *arte povera* movement, which emerged in the 1970s and is characterized by the use of humble materials, although the art—perhaps in spite of its intentions—often tends to look elegant. When Ace held a Kounellis retrospective, it disarmingly included some of his non–*arte povera* productions—large, angular metal sculptures that could have been the works of a different artist. A confrontation with this departure from Kounellis's familiar work was unavoidable, as visitors passing through the central hall had to navigate around the sculptures' ungainly appendages.

Since everything here is of Brobdingnagian proportions, you mustn't be surprised when you step into the bathroom. The gallery-size space in basic gray has a bank of four low-to-the-ground toilets on one wall, urinals on another, and a sink. Lock the door behind you. It's lonely in there. And try to relax.

AMERICAN FINE ARTS COLIN DE LAND FINE ART

CONCEPTUAL ART IN ALL MEDIA

22 WOOSTER STREET,
BETWEEN GRAND AND CANAL STREETS
(212) 941-0401
TUESDAY THROUGH SATURDAY,
NOON TO 6 P.M.

Seriously hip and with some political messages in the mix, this artists' favorite was founded in 1988. The gallery, located in SoHo's lower reaches just above Canal Street, in an unassuming building with a less assuming entrance, is easy to miss the first time you visit. It's certainly not out of the way, though. A block from the Drawing Center (the energetic and imaginative nonprofit exhibition space); several doors down from the lively gallery Basilico Fine Arts; and around the corner from the Art Store, which sells books, magazines, and well-designed gifts, the gallery is also close to a slew of reasonably priced SoHo restaurants, including the popular Lucky Strike bistro.

Much of what you'll see at this gallery is not so much about being pretty (though it just may be) as it is about ideas—that is, it's conceptual art. Among the artists exhibited here is the quirky funny-man John Waters, best known for the raunchy, subversive films he directs and acts in—like *Polyester* and *Hairspray.* Here he can be seen in the guise of photographer, with his witty and sometimes sad takes on people and seamy city streets. Mark Dion is far more earnest. His installations deal with natural history and efforts at classification. They appear to offer a behind-the-scenes glimpse at the workings of natural-history museums. There's a lot of creepy-looking stuff in bottles and shelves full of labeled specimens. Dion's friend and fellow natural-history buff Alexis Rockman has exhibited projects here, too. He approaches the subject from the synthetic rather than the analytic side, often drawing inspiration from the dioramas at natural-history museums. While he is best known for his brightly colored hyperreal paintings, where the likes of worms and insects assume disproportionately large dimensions, at American Fine Arts he has turned to installation art, presenting an enormous, as-close-to-real-as-possible stuffed (if not taxidermied) bear, for example, among his props.

Meanwhile, artists calling themselves AC2K use the gallery to show "art" that's critical of the art world, attacking its commercialism, in particular, and the power of the market. It could be biting the hand that feeds it, but maybe that hand likes to be bitten. Who knows? This is an unslick place, with offices and work space in the back. It shows the projects of many artists whom it doesn't necessarily represent, and it encourages experimentation.

ART RESOURCES TRANSFER

CONTEMPORARY ART, PUBLISHER, AND BOOKSTORE

210 ELEVENTH AVENUE, ROOM 403,

BETWEEN 24TH AND 25TH STREETS

(212) 691-5956

TUESDAY THROUGH SUNDAY,

11 A.M. TO 6 P.M.

Art Resources Transfer, Inc./A.R.T. Press is like no other gallery in the city. Founded and run by William Bartman, a longtime publisher of books and prints, this eclectic, eccentric exhibition space and bookstore offers something for everyone. The nonprofit enterprise shows and sells artists' books, prints, and objects produced in multiple editions; paintings and sculptures; exhibition catalogues; children's books; and gift items. Prices for the artwork remain much in this stratosphere, generally between $100 and $5,000.

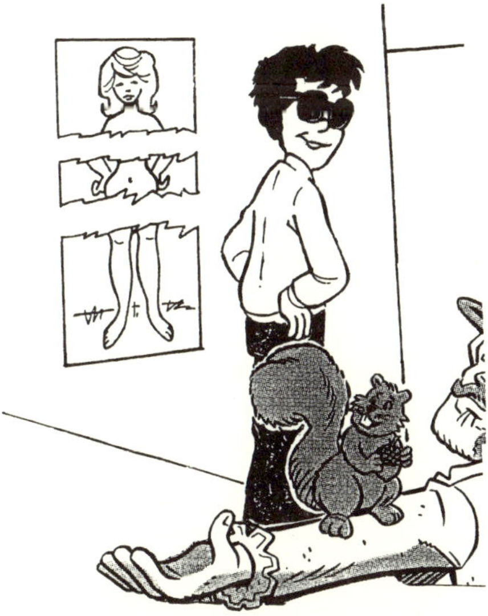

The irrepressible Bartman, who gads about flashing his wooden leg, is always juggling several shows at once: in three project rooms, the bookshop, and in the hallway. In the 1999/2000 season alone, he is exhibiting 79 artists. These range from the abstract painters Vija Celmins and Andy Spence to installationist Mike Kelley (known for his teddy bears), and photographer Laurie Simmons.

In an ongoing series called Conversations, Bartman invites two artists to exhibit together in one project space, establishing a dialogue through their work. In one, abstractionists Gwenn Thomas and Peggy Cyphers "discuss" what Thomas calls "narrative abstraction." Both artists work with various abstract shapes and styles that become their visual vocabulary. Cyphers presents oil paintings with layered images, such as washes topped by linear drawings, whereas Thomas makes collages—out of felt, for example—and then processes them as ink-jet or iris prints, which she mounts on canvas. With Thomas's layering, the final artwork is actually a reproduction. You can pick up printouts of the artists' actual conversations at the front desk.

The bookstore offers the art community—artists, art professionals, writers—a 25 percent discount on all books except A.R.T. Press's own publications, which sell at a 50 percent discount. Among the most notable of these is *Conversations,* in which portrait painter Chuck Close has conversations with 24 of his subjects.

And, that's not all. Everyone is welcome to attend the frequent artists' talks, book signings, and readings, as well as fund-raising art auctions. Stop in, too, just to nibble on cookies and hang out and chat with Bartman.

Peter Blum

99 Wooster Street,

between Prince and Spring streets

(212) 343-0441

Tuesday through Friday,

10 a.m. to 6 p.m.;

Saturday 11 a.m. to 6 p.m.

European and American painting, sculpture, and conceptual art

For a bit of European class, drop into the Peter Blum gallery. Here in this minimalistic, deep-set rectangular box, Blum applies his Swiss sensibility to the way he shows a surprisingly eclectic range of art that tends to be elegant and disciplined. Here you might find the sculpture and drawings of Toronto-born artist David Rabinowitch, whose strongly Minimalist, intellectually highfalutin sculptures are often based on math, music, and various philosophical and scientific concepts, or the installations of Barbara Bloom, known for her interiors, such as *Narcissism,* a roomful of objects bearing her name or image.

The grande dame of women artists, octogenarian Louise Bourgeois, exhibits here not only her installations (cagelike rooms full of dark and surreal dream imagery) but also her prints, which have been produced by Blum. The dealer was long known as a publisher of artists' books and prints before he opened the gallery. Now Blum shows work in many media, from painting, like portraits or details of leafy trees by the Pop art star Alex Katz (known best for his flat, nonperspectival depictions of his family and social set), to large works on paper, like the repetitive patterns of Philip Taaffe, to the stunning geometric paintings of the Switzerland-based Helmut Federle.

It's unlikely that you would expect to find anything like the Japanese conceptual artist Yukinori Yanagi's ant flags here. Plastic boxes are filled with colored sand in patterns reproducing national flags and are hung on the wall, connected to one another by tunnels. The ants, traveling from flag to flag, contaminate (or enrich) the patterns as they move the sand about, leading to some interesting international alliances. Yanagi works with ants from different regions, and guess what? He finds that some work harder than others.

Another Japanese artist, Yayoi Kusama, has shown some real career longevity. A figure on the Happenings and Pop art scene in the 1960s, Kusama has passed in and out of obscurity. Now she's back in full view. Working out of her studio in a psychiatric hospital in Tokyo, Kusama uses a wide range of media, from plastic blobs to mirrors and film, producing brilliantly colored and compulsively patterned paintings, objects, and installations. Recently, at the same time she was the subject of a large retrospective at the Museum of Modern Art, she showed her small, jewel-toned works on paper at Peter Blum. The gallery celebrated the opening with a tea ceremony.

Mary Boone

745 Fifth Avenue, 4th floor,
between 57th and 58th streets
(212) 752-2929
Tuesday through Friday,
10 A.M. to 6 P.M.;
Saturday, 10 A.M. to 5 P.M.

Contemporary paintings, drawings, and sculpture

Anyone who knows the smallest amount about New York's contemporary-art scene will probably have heard of Mary Boone. In business since 1977—indeed, one of the pioneers of SoHo—the high-profile Boone has handled some of the hottest figures of the high-flying eighties. Of those, the painters Ross Bleckner, known for his impeccably crafted and atmospheric abstractions, and Eric Fischl, who disconcerts and fascinates viewers with

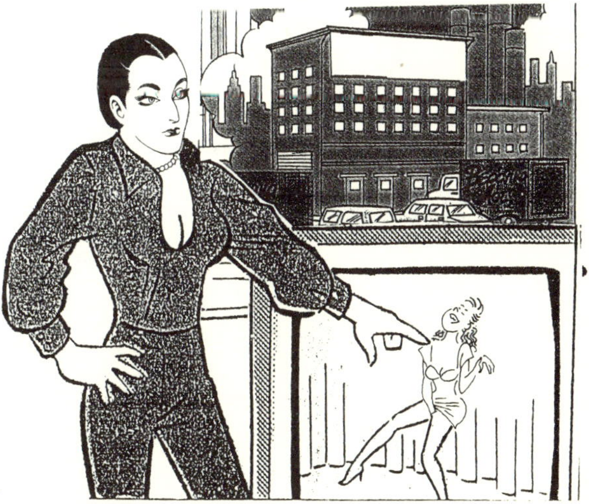

intense, often sexually charged psychological dramas, are still with her. Others have strayed to blue-chip galleries elsewhere but have been replaced by a new, international breed of young talents. This group includes the hyperrealist painter Damian Loeb, whose frighteningly aggressive, canvas-filling close-ups have been stealing some recent scenes. The gallery also presents curated shows of artists engaged in photography, video, and installation art. Among them are Britain's Turner Prize–winning Sam Taylor-Wood, whose videos focus on sexuality and intense psychological moments.

Boone decamped from SoHo a few years ago, moving up to the more corporate, collector-rich reaches of Fifth Avenue, where she currently inhabits a few large, spare, windowless rooms in the same building with the McKee and Forum galleries. There, besides the young and new, she also shows more established artists, such as the African American Leonardo Drew, whose large installations are often composed of burnt wood, rags, and other detritus. These are artfully built into attractive sculptures and wall pieces that leave viewers wondering how such disturbing materials can be so physically appealing.

Obviously this is not a gallery that can be ignored, and word has it that Boone is soon opening a second space in Chelsea, so that the gallery's young and edgiest artists can be seen among their own kind in warehouse-style digs.

JANET BORDEN

CONTEMPORARY PHOTOGRAPHY

560 BROADWAY, 6TH FLOOR,
CORNER OF PRINCE STREET
(212) 431-0166
TUESDAY THROUGH SATURDAY,
11 A.M. TO 5 P.M.

Situated in the same building with the pricey and delectable Dean & DeLuca food emporium, the Janet Borden gallery is an airy haven for photography and photo-related art. In business since 1988, Borden has developed a varied stable of well-known and imaginative photographers.

Among the dozen or so she represents is Tina Barney, who is most famous for her grimly insightful glimpses into affluent, bored New England family life. Jan Groover shows images that have developed from her vividly colored still lifes of the 1980s to her current, more nostalgic images of landscapes.

Larry Sultan reveals his perceptive eye in photographs of, for example, his family in Florida. In a fascinating, discomfiting series, he turns a parodic yet compassionate and affectionate lens on his parents, living the clichéd retired life, as they stand around the pool or sit at the breakfast table. He captures them as symbols of a way of life and of a stage in life—Grant Wood's *American Gothic* for the leisure class.

Striking a boldly surreal note in a different key is the photographer-sculptor Sandy Skoglund, who dazzles audiences with such work as a gigantic, gallery-packing jelly-bean-and-butterfly installation, composed of larger-than-life-size, candy-covered sculpted figures (women with their heads on backward and men with their heads on straight) caught seemingly mid-dance on a floor of jelly beans. As backdrop for the drama, a wall full of realistic-looking butterflies fluttered their wings, while hanging elsewhere are photographs of what you were seeing. It's easy to imagine that the jelly-bean people are engaged in a piece of performance art—a dance of life—and that they could be eaten up at any time. Standout works in Skoglund's career—acid-colored photographs of staged tableaus, such as a child's nursery, with dream images of mammoth fish floating by, and woodsy scenes with orange squirrels on the ground—have also appeared at the gallery, with both the installation and photographs of it on view.

One of the first major so-called mall buildings for art, 560 Broadway houses a varied array of gallery spaces. Borden's neighbors in the building range from Lennon, Weinberg, which represents a solid core of mid-career abstract American painters and sculptors, to Nolan/Eckman, which shows European and American works on paper. Werner Kramarsky, one of the city's most devoted and sophisticated collectors, who tirelessly supports young artists working mostly on paper in the abstract-minimalist vein, also has offices in the building, which he periodically opens for exhibitions. You might want to check out A/D, a gallery devoted to artist-designed furniture, rugs, wallpaper, and even glassware.

Bound & Unbound

601 West 26th Street, 12th floor,
between Eleventh and Twelfth avenues
(212) 463-7348
Tuesday through Saturday,
Noon to 6 p.m.

Bookshop/exhibition space for postwar avant-garde art

Something of a secret pleasure, this unfussy book collector's retreat deals in all manner of ephemera, including gallery announcements, pamphlets, postcards, Fluxus materials, posters, and, of course, books. It is also situated in one of Chelsea's choicest structures—the Art Deco Starrett Lehigh Building.
Visual puns abound in this cozy but commodious gallery with a wall of windows forming a grid through which to view Hudson River activity, lower Manhattan, and New Jersey. The place still has the air of a traditional rare-book shop rather than one of Chelsea chic. It's a browser's paradise, with boxes to sort through, vitrines, shelves, and tables covered with stuff—as well as a comfy sofa and chairs.

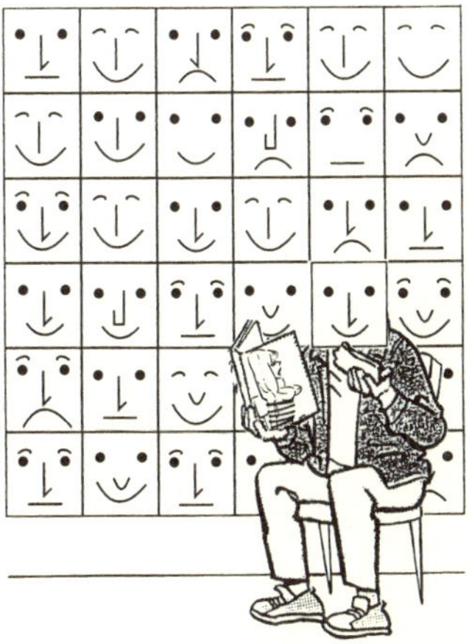

A natural in this gallery's purview is mail art, a curious genre that has recently received much attention in the work of the late Ray Johnson.

Mail art—simply, art sent through the mail—becomes a kind of public art, unvetted by galleries, curators, or advisers. It operates outside any commercial network—at least, at first. It is not treated as precious matter, since it gets stamped, mangled, and stuffed into boxes, and its recipients often don't know why they've been chosen or that what they are receiving is actually "art," so there's a democratic quality to it all. Eventually the drawings, collages, and miscellany may be accepted as fine art and sold at appropriate—or even inappropriate—prices, but they have come in the back door and established their value on their own.

This spirit characterizes what you'll find here, where much of the work focuses on the interface between the verbal and the plastic arts. There are many examples of concrete poetry, where the configurations of words and letters form a picture of a subject, providing a visual and mental image.

Lawrence Weiner is a prime practitioner. Among the most important conceptual artists today, Weiner specializes in words and geometry, making many works on paper in large, unlimited editions that are popularly accessible, often funny and intellectually provocative. His wordplays include works like a poster for the Dia Center for the Arts. It features the word "displacement" printed above and below two squares that have been cut out of the paper and are separated by a printed ampersand; in this way, words and design speak in unison.

Other visual punsters whose work shows up here are the late Belgian artist Marcel Broodthaers, known for his buckets of mussel shells and suitcases full of eggshells, and the British conceptualist Ian Hamilton Finlay, whose works—often prints, drawings, and objects in multiples—focus on nature, classical culture, and neoclassical French history and art, all translated into the language of contemporary Conceptualism. A clear example of his work is a print titled *Two Landscapes of the Sublime,* picturing an image of Niagara Falls beside an image of a guillotine, both in the same configuration.

Owned by Barbara Moore, a former rare-book dealer, Bound & Unbound is conveniently next door to Jan Van Der Donk Rare Books, which specializes in 20th-century avant-garde art, design, and photography.

Gavin Brown's Enterprise Corp.

436 West 15th Street,

Between Ninth and Tenth Avenues

(212) 627-5258

Tuesday through Saturday,

10 A.M. to 6 P.M.

For fun and funky fare as well as serious, more mainstream work by artists on the younger side, check out Gavin Brown. Providing a base for some and a springboard for other cheeky figures, Brown has recently set up shop on one of the latest-to-be-settled blocks, at 436 West 15th Street, between the West Village and Chelsea. The meatpacking district is just a block below, and the big Chelsea Market, where you can get everything from fresh seafood fare for eating on the spot to flowers to weekend tango lessons, is immediately to the north.

Since his beginning in 1994 on the western outskirts of SoHo, Brown has been a pioneering presence in out-of-the-way locales. Now the British-born gallery owner may have actually landed himself in a soon-to-be center. But just in case you haven't noticed the neighborhood's chicness in the making, the gallery has opened up its own bar hangout in an adjoining space.

Step way into this deep-set gallery, and you might see photographs by Steven Pippin, whose pictures—some taken by a camera inside a washing machine capturing the artist Andrea Zittel running back and forth naked—often recall the work of 19th-century master Eadweard

Muybridge. Also in Brown's stable is the young Los Angeles artist Laura Owen, whose lively abstract paintings juggle the styles of several of her contemporaries, including the impastoed squiggles of Jonathan Lasker, but the colors and combinations of elements and allusions she uses are unmistakably hers. Another painter who shows here is the more mid-career British artist Peter Doig, whose large paintings that combine abstraction and the figure tend to be rich, atmospheric, and somehow threatening meditations on landscape—a toppled figure in snowy mountains, for example.

Rob Pruitt, by contrast, simply insists on engaging you. He offers suggestions and instructions and fills the gallery with examples of work you can make yourself out of everyday materials. His show "101 Art Ideas You Can Do Yourself"—which, wrote the critic Katie Clifford in *ARTnews,* "was part Martha Stewart industriousness,

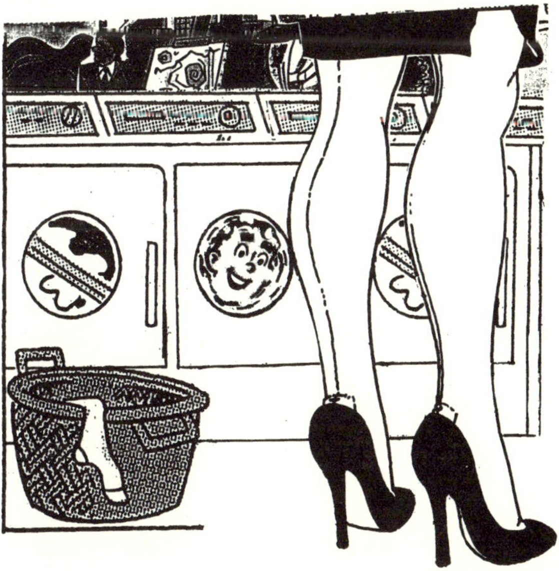

part Bob Ross (of TV's "Joy of Painting") warm-and-fuzzy encouragement, and generally high Duchampian antics"—included such ideas as making art with make-up, showing as an example a puppy created out of mascara and blusher.

Rirkrit Tiravanija, on the other hand, doesn't ask us to take his advice; rather, he urges us to join him. The conceptual artist, who might just be cooking a meal as part of a performance, most recently reproduced his life in the gallery—bathtub and all. His wife, painter Elizabeth Peyton, is represented by the gallery as well, where she shows her almost traditional portraits of pop celebrities (Kurt Cobain, for one) painted in disarmingly acidic colors. Very modish.

Expect the improbable at Gavin Brown, and go to the openings there—everyone else does.

CHEIM & READ

521 WEST 23RD STREET,
BETWEEN TENTH AND ELEVENTH AVENUES
(212) 242-7727
TUESDAY THROUGH SATURDAY,
10 A.M. TO 6 P.M.

CONTEMPORARY PAINTING, SCULPTURE, AND PHOTOGRAPHY

A relative newcomer, but only in a way, Cheim & Read opened in 1996. The owners, however, John Cheim and Howard Read, were long associated with the distinguished Robert Miller Gallery, and many of the artists you'll see here are or were also affiliated with Miller. Many big guns show at this gallery, like the never-more-popular Louise Bourgeois (who in her 80s has proved herself stationed prominently at the forefront of the contemporary-art scene), as well as important mid-career artists like Lynda Benglis, who paints and sculpts gelatinous blobs, makes sensual surreal films, and has even applied her esthetic to jewelry making; the abstract painter Louise Fishman, known for her large and inventive gestures; and Richmond Burton, whose complex, vividly colored abstract paintings are stikingly beautiful.

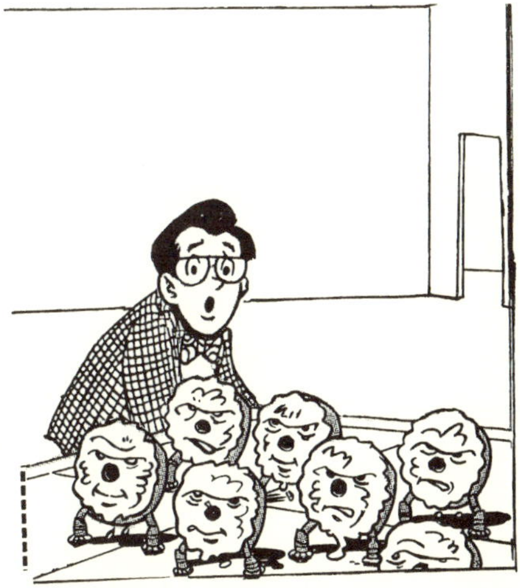

So are those of Spanish artist

Juan Uslé. His nearly infinite variations on abstract painting—from layered gridlike canvases to a big, stark, red composition with a seductive, unidentifiable black shape in the middle—can be seen along with spare, sharply defined photographs that explore reality and abstraction and also negotiate with the seductive power of color and composition.

Besides shows of individual artists, the gallery offers some imaginative combinations of historical works with modern and contemporary ones. One exhibition, put together by the French curator Jean Clair, matched up the 18th-century caricature busts—grotesque studies of temperament—of Austrian sculptor Franz Xaver Messerschmidt with the excruciatingly contorted figures of the modern British painter Francis Bacon and a small Bourgeois "room" with mirrors and a disembodied arm and hand to be glimpsed through various apertures in the structure. It was Bourgeois who noted her own kinship with those two artists.

This gallery still seems very fresh, taking on new artists, showing unfamiliar work in different media by known ones, and coming up with some unusual aesthetic concoctions.

Note well: The bathroom here is attractive and accessible, and you don't have to ask for a key.

Paula Cooper

534 West 21st Street,
Between Tenth and Eleventh Avenues
(212) 255-1105
Tuesday through Saturday,
10 A.M. to 6 P.M.

Contemporary paintings, sculpture, works on paper, and video

Paula Cooper, owner of one of the city's best-loved galleries, is known for her independence, loyalty to artists, and unwillingness to be an art-world groupie. A decade ago she told an interviewer, "I don't like art dealers very much, and I don't enjoy the selling of art—practically everything you talk about always comes back to money."

Obviously this attitude hasn't hurt. Her cathedral to art, built in Chelsea in 1996 in a former storage building for ducts and ventilators, testifies to her success—and taste. Designed by one of the art world's most sensitive and ubiquitous architects, Richard Gluckman (his firm also did the Whitney Museum's new galleries), the Paula Cooper gallery exhibits work by a number of blue-chip contemporary artists, including the Minimalist Carl Andre, best known for his floor installations in such materials as brick, slate, and copper, and the late Tony Smith, whose manly monolithic sculptures—no matter their size—take command of their environs. Another sculptor, Robert Grosvenor, who has been with Cooper for many years, also favors large, often spare sculptures that relate to the landscape or architecture.

On a far different note are the drawings and sets that Robert Wilson designs for his avant-garde operas. The black-and-white drawings by this multidimensional artist are expressive abstractions that tend to be architectural and lyrical.

Younger artists, too, are being increasingly represented by the gallery. Among them, Zoe Leonard, who is still in her 30s. Her installations deal with nature, natural history, the museums devoted to those subjects, and the people who visit those institutions.

The controversial photographer Andres Serrano—most famous, or infamous, for his *Piss Christ,* made with his own urine—aims to shock, but he does it through seduction. His disturbing, sexually provocative, or simply very frank images (of people in morgues or naked elderly people) are startlingly sharp and arresting.

Unsettling—or better, confounding—in other ways are the works of the Conceptualist Robert Gober. An example of his sometimes macabre post-Pop-art sensibility is his famous fully-clothed disembodied leg sticking out of a wall.

Since her pioneering days in SoHo, where in 1968 she was among the first to open a gallery, Cooper has championed some of the most important contemporary artists.

DANZIGER

851 MADISON AVENUE,
BETWEEN 70TH AND 71ST STREETS
(212) 734-5300
TUESDAY THROUGH SATURDAY,
10 A.M. TO 6 P.M.

19TH- AND 20TH-CENTURY PHOTOGRAPHY

Since its establishment on Prince Street in SoHo, Danziger has maintained a central position in the blue-chip photography market, exhibiting and selling distinguished vintage work as well as images by the likes of present-day photo luminary Annie Leibovitz, chronicler of the fashion and celebrity worlds and a *Vanity Fair* magazine staple.

A couple of years ago the gallery moved uptown to its current commodious second-floor space, with three main viewing rooms, close to its upscale institutional and private collectors and to stylish retailers Yves Saint Laurent, Ralph Lauren, and Prada.

Openings here can be star-studded, in part because these are the people Leibovitz and other gallery artists focus on. At the same time, many serious collectors frequent the gallery for its mainstream images and vintage fare. But its contemporary offerings aren't always so obvious and predictable. While the gallery favors portrayals of faces and places, some of these are decidedly unconventional, like those of the Mexican artist Luis Gonzalez Palma, whose subject is usually himself. He superimposes images one upon the other as he explores his own identity. Susan Derges's large photos, each print unique, from her "River Taw Series," for example, are also strange—very painterly depictions of segments of nature, such as a bunch of leaves on a tree, in otherworldly tones of green.

Danziger usually has old and new works on view simultaneously, and the former include many by the most important practitioners, among them Henri Cartier-Bresson, Jacques-Henri Lartigue, Cecil Beaton, and Harold Edgerton. The gallery represents these estates exclusively, although it also has works available by other persistent high rollers, such as Ansel Adams, Richard Avedon, and Julia Margaret Cameron.

DEITCH PROJECTS

CONTEMPORARY ARTISTS' PROJECTS

76 GRAND STREET,

BETWEEN WOOSTER AND GREENE STREETS

(212) 343-7300

TUESDAY THROUGH SATURDAY,

NOON TO 6 P.M.

Soho's Deitch Projects is, without a doubt, one of the foremost launching pads for a very talented cast of emerging international artists and a showcase for some established ones. In a former garage on Grand Street, previously occupied by the beloved Fawbush Gallery, Deitch exhibits an unusually broad selection of mostly avant-garde works by such notables as the Japanese artist Mariko Mori, who continues to thrill her audience with her childlike, hyperreal and surreal video images

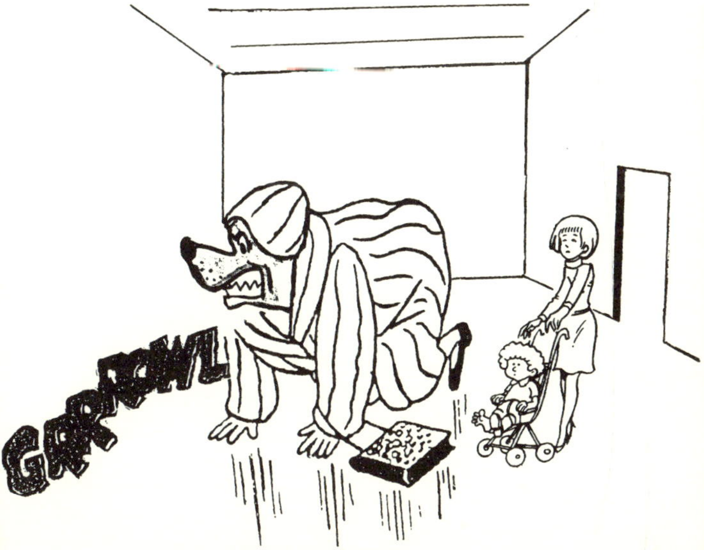

portraying some fairy-tale, and Jeff Koons, who remains one of the most pop Pop artists of all, with his preposterously outsize renditions of toys and household objects and even a several-stories-high terrier puppy made of flowers.

The gallery also shows some interesting lesser-known figures, such as African artist Malick Sidibé, who presents black-and-white photographs documenting social life in his native Bamako from the 1960s to recent times, and reinforces them with larger-than-life sculptures in bright colors of couples dancing and mimicking the activities in the photographs.

Although he opened the space in 1996, owner Jeffrey Deitch has been a force in the art world for many years, working as a curator and an art adviser, both corporate and private. He has cannily rounded up his band of hot and controversial young figures working in all media. The offerings here are happily unpredictable, since Deitch himself not only exhibits work but helps fund projects. Bring the kids when architects Ada Tolla and Giuseppe Lignano, a duo calling themselves LOT/EK, cut-up sections of a petroleum-tank trailer whose interiors have been outfitted with rubber tubing, a TV, and a remote control. (They can climb in for comfy viewing.) Or when Teresita Fernandez turns one gallery room into a swimming pool, with video-green lighting for atmosphere.

But leave the children at home, perhaps, when the naked, caged Russian conceptual artist Oleg Kulik literally lives like a dog for several weeks, barking and biting those who provoke him. Here you can tap into the Zeitgeist, though you may not be able to categorize what you witness.

Feigen Contemporary

Contemporary Art in All Media

535 West 20th Street,
Between Tenth and Eleventh Avenues
(212) 929-0500
Tuesday through Saturday,
11 a.m. to 6 p.m.

This two-story gallery, a branch of the uptown Feigen institution that specializes in Old Masters and more traditional modern art, made its foray into Chelsea a couple of years ago. It is actually a reincarnation of the now defunct Chicago branch of Feigen, also called Feigen Contemporary.

The enormous space has essentially three viewing areas: the entry, the main gallery, and a basement for exhibitions and storage. Into it all go works by such artists as the consummate Pop star James Rosenquist, whose billboard-style paintings of a commercial and technologically advanced America still captivate viewers. Rosenquist's recent works are in the familiar deep pastel tones that imbue his images with both a tropical and an other-planetary feel. Pictures of airplanes, lightbulbs, canned goods, and women with toothpaste smiles are painted so sleekly—and flatly—and in such densely patterned backgrounds that they succumb to a kind of abstraction.

So do the young artist Jeremy Blake's videos. He explores interiors, as in his series "Bungalow 8," where the camera moves very slowly through modernist rooms that are generally devoid of people. The aqua tones create an air of another reality, and the languid motion of the camera another time zone. Blake plugs in to the current appreciation of neomodernism, including L.A. interiors of the fifties and sixties and the films of that period both here and in Europe.

Uncompromisingly abstract investigations characterize the works of a number of gallery artists, Shirley Kaneda among them. Kaneda could be considered a true post-modernist, making pastiches of numerous clashing and contradictory patterns in each of her painstakingly perfect painted canvases. The compositions take viewers aback, looking as they do like a very stylish display of clothing fabrics.

Often the gallery presents curated group shows, with affiliated and unaffiliated artists, that are assembled around a theme, such as one on the contemporary manifestations of abstraction. That exhibition featured artists like Christopher Wool, with his hieroglyph-like markings in black on white canvases; Dona Nelson, an early user of the now fashionable gel-like paint in unmodulated and opaque pastel tones; and Matthew Ritchie, whose puzzles and maps of patterns wend their way from wall to floor.

Feigen also represents the painter Charles Spurrier, whose lush, jewel–toned abstract confections drip with seduction and mystery.

Feigen still seems like a young gallery, offering unexpected perspectives.

Ronald Feldman

Modern and Contemporary Art

31 Mercer Street,
between Grand and Canal streets
(212) 226-3232
Tuesday through Saturday,
10 a.m. to 6 p.m.

At close to 30 years old, the Ronald Feldman gallery has assembled a solid, international cast of some 35 important contemporary artists. And as much as the work you might see here varies, the common denominator is a focus on ideas—social, scientific, political, cultural. Their purveyors are the likes of Ida Applebroog, a longtime feminist and devoted Minimalist artist, and the Russian Conceptualist Ilya Kabakov. Applebroog works in her signature style of linear drawings in comic-strip-like boxes, telling personal stories and strange, disconcerting dream sequences. Sometimes she turns them into installations with objects and separate canvases extending onto the floor; at this point they become installations. Some of her works explore the Holocaust and concentration camps; others look at family life and city living, making us all feel like voyeurs as we peer through her windows.

Kabakov and the Russian team of Komar & Melamid bring their pasts into the present in very different ways. Kabakov still looks back occasionally with claustrophobic installations of art- and book-filled rooms—asylums, libraries—that are both real and fantastic reconstructions of another culture. States of mind are made physical. Komar & Melamid engage in a range of parody, social criticism, and simply goofy carryings-on. They take public-opinion polls to determine what various cultures like most in paintings and then produce paintings that fit the descriptions: for example, Americans like the color blue, landscapes, and historical figures. (The two have also opened an art school in Cincinnati, Ohio—for elephants.)

The work of the late German artist Joseph Beuys, with his politically and emotionally charged works made of felt, fat, and stone, also puts in appearances, lending an air of earnestness and melancholy.

This large, comfortable, multichambered lower SoHo space—a short skip from Pearl Paint on Canal Street, the pantheon of art supplies and office sundries—can even accommodate mini-factory productions, like the blob-making machine of Roxy Paine that pumps out a white, congealing gook, which turns into a steady sequence of amorphous sculptures on a simple conveyor belt.

When the Puerto Rican-born artist Pepón Osorio takes over the gallery with his over-the-top installations, he turns it into a kind of barrio carnival. His funny-and-serious constructed environments—such as a barbershop, a bedroom, or the scene of a crime—assembled out of gaudy and banal objects and stray bits of electronic gadgetry, including TV sets, invite visitors into an intense, concentrated, sophisticated, and portable Latin American world.

GAGOSIAN

136 WOOSTER STREET,
BETWEEN PRINCE AND HOUSTON STREETS
(212) 228-2828
TUESDAY THROUGH SATURDAY, 10 A.M. TO 6 P.M.

980 MADISON AVENUE,
BETWEEN 76TH AND 77TH STREETS
(212) 744-2313
TUESDAY THROUGH SATURDAY, 10 A.M. TO 6 P.M.

MODERN AND CONTEMPORARY ART IN ALL MEDIA

Since its establishment in 1991 in two spaces—uptown, in the very tony former Sotheby's auction-house building, and downtown, behind SoHo-chic garage doors that can roll up for large-sculpture shows—Gagosian has specialized in high-end, high-profile figures as well as museum-style, guest-curated exhibitions of works by such artists as Peter Paul Rubens and Arshile Gorky.

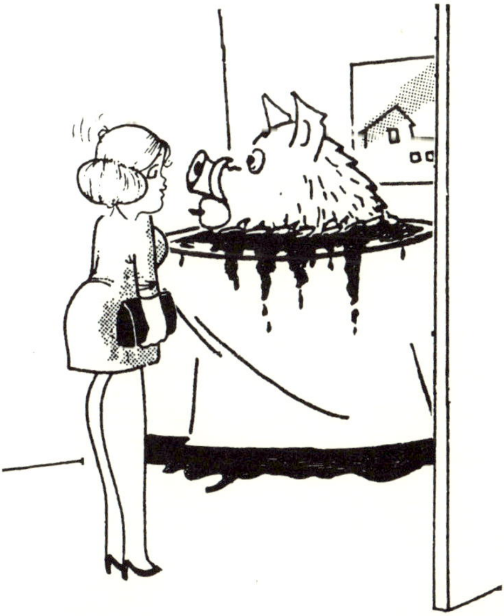

Perhaps it's the grandness of these spaces that allows for big, dramatic statements, but even the more conceptual artists Larry Gagosian represents make some pretty theatrical works. Especially downtown, the gallery often becomes a stage for some outlandish sets. In fact, it's hard to beat Gagosian for sheer spectacle: There's the British bad-boy sensation Damien Hirst's cut-up cows and swimming-pool-size, cigarette-butt-filled ashtrays, and those other British provocateurs Dinos and Jake Chapman's androgynous boys and girls connected by bits of genitalia where you'd least expect to find them, and the Glaswegian video artist Douglas Gordon's clip of a well-known scene from the movie *Taxi Driver* shown on facing screens in dialogue with itself.

You're also likely to find artists working in more traditional media, namely, painting and sculpture. Enter the uptown building, on Madison Avenue between 76th and 77th streets; walk through the large lobby to the elevator at the far left; and take it to the sixth floor. Here in this monument to Minimalist decor you might see Philip Taaffe's exacting, repetitive patterns based on nature and architecture; Francesco Clemente's luxuriant, sensual paintings; Ellen Gallager's paintings with tiny symbols of race and oppression encoded in the patterns of her meticulous, apparent abstractions; or works by the generous-gestured, expressionistic American sculptor Mark di Suvero, who shows uptown, downtown, and all about town.

Gagosian also represents the late David Smith, whose bold, Cubist-Constructivist-painterly constructions defined a moment when sculpture could enjoy being playful and serious at the same time, and the high Minimalist Richard Serra, who is regarded by many as the foremost sculptor of our times.

Sandra Gering

476 Broome Street, 2nd floor,

between Greene and Wooster streets

(212) 226-8195

Tuesday through Saturday,

10 A.M. to 6 P.M.

Art, especially conceptual art, in all media by American, European, Asian, and Latin American artists

From the mechanized structures of Taro Chiezo to the video sculptures of Matthew McCaslin and the computer-game narratives of Kathleen Ruiz, which allow viewers to probe and participate in an understanding of the mental state of her brother, the Sandra Gering Gallery regularly and heartily succumbs to the lure of technological innovation. And best of all—or worst, depending on who you are—much of it is interactive. But no one will scold you if you refuse to don virtual-reality gear or click on a mouse; you can always watch someone else do it.

Sandra Gering first ran a quiet contemporary gallery out of her Greenwich Village town house. But here, in a narrow strip of rooms on Broome Street, up a creaky elevator to the second floor, it's an entirely different story.

You might find among the intriguing works here, Meghan Boody's near-surreal, manipulated Cibachrome photographs mimicking Renaissance canvases. Her series "Henry's Wives" treats in painstaking and comic detail tableaus from the lives of Henry's six wives—each a distinct archetype, but all, as Boody notes, "unlucky in love." Her own image stands in for that of the wives.

McCaslin's video installations, as the critic and artist Carol Diehl has put it, "are for those who have happy memories of watching the test pattern on TV." Stacking and connecting bunches of TV screens, McCaslin will sometimes use the same image in different colors on many screens, creating a new composite image, such as four rows of four screens with eyeballs blinking out of sequence. Decorative, funny, or socially critical, McCaslin's work has been making appearances at various venues about town.

Another gallery artist is Dove Bradshaw, a sculptor who experiments with the effects of nature on her materials—for example, a hunk of white marble with a pyrite rock on top leaking a rust stain, like blood, down the face of the white stone.

But no need to explain more; you can find most of Gering's offerings on the Web, and some works have been designed exclusively for the cyberworld. Just call up gering@interport.net.

Barbara Gladstone

Art in all media, especially conceptual art

515 West 24th Street,
between Tenth and Eleventh Avenues
(212) 206-9300
Tuesday through Saturday,
10 a.m. to 6 p.m.

The Barbara Gladstone gallery has established itself as a top-notch venue for a serious international group of mostly conceptual artists. There is not much of an emerging-artists scene, here; for that you'll have to check out some of the galleries down the block, like Andrea Rosen and Luhring Augustine, which have "project" rooms for that purpose. Nevertheless, a recent sign-on is the much-in-the-news Iranian conceptual photographer Shirin Neshat.

This is a large gallery, the first you come upon when you're walking west from Tenth Avenue and just past a big garage restoring and selling used Mercedes-Benzes. While the interior spaces—four different-size areas on the main floor—don't flow particularly logically into one another, the layout does allow the gallery to show large and small works, installation art, and videos as well as paintings and works on paper in areas best suited to their scale.

American artists as different as Richard Prince, Matthew Barney, and Vito Acconci can be seen here. Prince is known for his post–Pop art and kitschy cartoon-and-hackneyed-joke paintings with touches of computer-generated squiggles. Sometimes the jokes stand alone on the canvas in simple print; other times they're scrawled among painted rocky landscapes.

Among Matthew Barney's often grandiose enterprises, concerned with various issues of identity, are slick, surreal films with androgynous figures cross-dressing and sometimes camping it up in homage to (and as a parody of) Hollywood–how is was and will be. His other installations have consisted of enormous, room-filling unidentifiable objects tangled together, looking like a forest of medical apparatus or gymnasium equipment. As for Vito Acconci, who is often included in curated group shows throughout the city, you never know what you'll find. A provocateur in the seventies who filmed himself engaging in unseemly acts of self-abuse, Acconci has come to be a play-vocateur (if such can be said) with his gigantic sculptural installations, such as his umbrella breasts, and public-art furnishings, like the longitudinal half of a concrete car as a bus-stop bench.

Among the international contingent, the Cuban-born KCHO (his real name is Alexis Leyva Machado) exhibits his canoes in many positions—sitting and hanging—and collaged with book pages, diary notes, letters, and the like. They express the plight of Cuban refugees and reflect on the passage of life in general.

The India-born, London-based artist Anish Kapoor makes exquisite, often dangerous work. In the intense colors of some sea urchins that lure their prey, Kapoor fashions otherworldly objects that could suggest small mountains and desert-sand configurations. But don't succumb to the seduction of these beautiful forms—the color can rub off. Once (but no longer) the pigment was even toxic. Now, that's real beauty.

Marian Goodman

Contemporary Art in All Media

24 West 57th Street, 4th floor,
between Fifth and Sixth Avenues
(212) 977-7160
Monday through Saturday,
10 A.M. to 6 P.M.

Long one of the most sophisticated venues in New York, the Marian Goodman gallery has a stable of principally conceptual artists—European and American—in the seemingly staid Gallery Building on West 57th Street. Goodman, who began in business in 1965 with her lively and eclectic Multiples gallery (which sold just that—prints, objects, even furniture) and opened as Marian Goodman in 1977, exhibits some of the best-known avant-garde artists worldwide. The German artist Anselm Kiefer does awesomely dramatic and monumental works in straw and other earthy, sometimes disturbing, materials; the American conceptual artist Lawrence Weiner is famous for his signs and word pieces (his little books, posters, pins, and other objects are available at prices almost anyone can

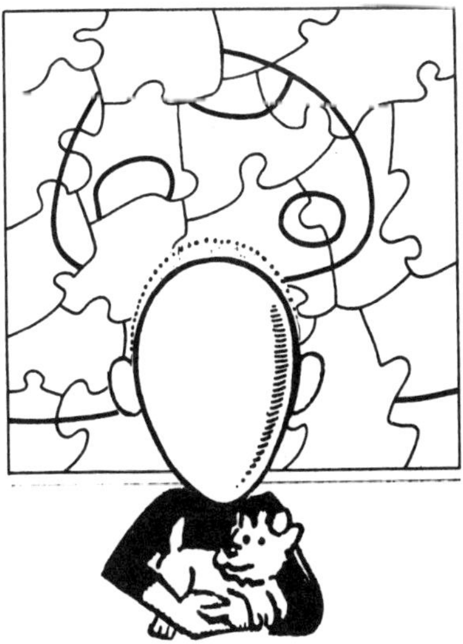

afford—which is their point); and Marcel Broodthaers, the late Belgium conceptual artist, filled suitcases and buckets, among other things, with eggshells and mussels. Broodthaers has been the subject of several shows at the gallery, which reproduced his personal museum of historical memorabilia and emblems.

Goodman presents work in all media, ranging from the German artist Rebecca Horn's mechanized contraptions that wiggle and do tricks (for example, her installation made of brass horns that emits hornish sounds—a multiple-pun machine) to the Spanish artist Juan Muñoz's life-size, gray brooding figures that move nearly imperceptibly and constitute a strange, mute community.

More direct are the photographs of the Canadian artist Jeff Wall and of the German Thomas Ruff. You feel as if you could almost step into Wall's light-box landscapes and interiors, such as one depicting a museum restoration with scaffolding and restorers at work, while Ruff's extremely close, unforgiving portraits let the subjects' faces fill the entire frame.

German Renaissance man Gerhard Richter is a regular scene-stealer here. The effects and techniques of his distinctive, wildly influential abstract and photo-based paintings reverberate in the work of a generation of artists worldwide.

The feel of this gallery is rather distant European, the majority of artists being German, and the staff particularly discreet. But if you walk down the hall to Goodman's south gallery, you'll usually find someone friendly to answer your questions—and lend you the key to the very nice rest rooms in the corridor.

Gorney Bravin + Lee

Contemporary Art in All Media

534 West 26th Street,

between Tenth and Eleventh Avenues

(212) 352-8372

Tuesday through Saturday,

10 a.m. to 6 p.m.

Gorney Bravin + Lee is a triumvirate formed in 1998 by Jay Gorney, the former owner of the Jay Gorney gallery, and Karin Bravin and John Post Lee, the former owners of the Bravin Post Lee gallery—two strong spaces for an imaginative assortment of artists. Now, thanks to their presence on one of Chelsea's ever-livelier buildings—joining the pioneering GreeneNaftali and recent arrivals Robert Miller and Nicole Klagsbrun at 526 West 26th and spaces like Pamela Auchincloss and Bound and Unbound at 601—visitors can experience a broad cross-section of contemporary currents.

Wide-ranging and quirky, the new gallery's artists include Sam Samore, who works in video and photography and specializes in grainy, blurred images of figures set in no apparent context. Samore establishes mystery in the dissolution of form and the sense of placelessness that prevails even as the subjects appear to interact.

Animals and nature take charge in the works of two very popular artists, William Wegman and Alexis Rockman. Wegman's stately weimaraners, photographed wearing outrageous, human-mimicking costumes and playing unsuspecting roles, turn up here, as do Rockman's vividly painted versions of natural-history-museum dioramas, with outsize earthworms and elephants and foliage dramatically intertwined.

In a cooler mode are the photographs of the Conceptualist Sarah Charlesworth, known for elegant, surreal images, and the work of the late abstract artist Moira Dryer, whose paintings and some sculpture still seem fresh and to the point.

The ever exuberant sculptor Jessica Stockholder's brilliant-colored constructions of all sizes turn the ideas of Action painting, 3-D, and Day-Glo otherworldly. Her multimedia extravaganzas look as if they could grow indefinitely, eventually subsuming their surroundings. The young painter Jennifer Reeves also does some lively abstract work, but she sticks to the canvas, using varying textures, like built-up squiggles of pigment, slightly reminiscent of the technique of painters like Jonathan Lasker and Laura Owen but set in a very different landscape and mindscape.

Adding to the diversity here are Charles LeDray's cute but chilling installations with tiny clothes in vitrines, Fabian Marcaccio's lush abstract paintings, and Catherine Opie's in-your-face photographs of members of various countercultures.

GREENE-NAFTALI

526 WEST 26 STREET, 8TH FLOOR,
BETWEEN TENTH AND ELEVENTH AVENUES
(212) 463-7770
TUESDAY THROUGH SATURDAY,
10 A.M. TO 6 P.M.

EMERGING INTERNATIONAL ARTISTS, WITH A FOCUS ON NEW YORK AND LOS ANGELES

It's almost like going over the meadow and through the woods to get to this hip space in one of upper Chelsea's converted factory buildings. Once you take the old-fashioned gated elevator with its real live attendant to the eighth floor, you'll find yourself navigating labyrinthine hallways. But arrows point the way, and then, voila!—you'll see GreeneNaftali's big glass doors and beyond them the wondrous expansive view from a wall of north-facing windows.

GreeneNaftali was certainly in the advance guard when it opened here, in 1995. Now, it's far from alone, to say the least. Many new and established galleries have moved in—along with artists' studios and art-related businesses. With the gallery-filled Art Deco Starrett Lehigh Building just a block farther west, 26th Street has become something of an art center in itself. You could easily spend a day exploring these two buildings alone.

At this gallery, you're likely to find everything from some of the most cutting edge, experimental work being done today internationally to just plain contemporary art, which encompasses abstract and figurative paintings and sculpture. Sometimes they're even shown all together, when densely covered walls of paintings by such mid-career abstractionists as Juan Uslé and Brice Marden are juxtaposed with video works, avant-garde handout literature-and-art magazines, and other ephemera. Carol Greene, the gallery's director and co-owner with Gloria Naftali, was formerly the director of the John Good gallery, an important venue for a generation of strong abstract artists. She has since extended her purview to take in adventuresome emerging international artists, who hang out at the gallery and work in all media, including new technological ones.

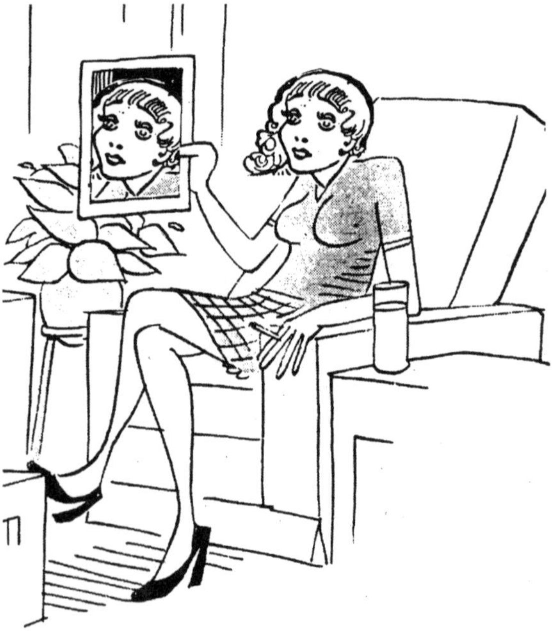

Things are always changing here, and that entails moving the walls around. You might feel that you're rarely in the same place twice. The variety of artwork comprises the familiar paintings of veteran Pop star Alex Katz and gallery artists Jacqueline Humphries, a talented colorist, who makes alluring abstract paintings, and the young Blake Rayne, whose canvases combine the figurative and the abstract and are concerned with light and shallow perspective—a kind of contemporary Impressionism. But the gallery also showcases the strange videos of British artist Lucy Gunning who, among other things captures herself on tape whinnying and pretending she is a horse. Another perspective on video that is less personal and more political is provided in the bright-colored graphics of Berliner Daniel Pflumm, who explores product logos by twisting and turning them to varying effects: CNN, for example, plays again and again in one guise or another while split-screen images on a neighboring screen show TV news commentators and guests in suspended conversation.

A witty look at the future was on the mind of Laura Emrick when she produced her sculptural installation *A Proposal for the First Museum of Mars.* The critic Kim Levin described it as "a love affair with the unearthly fluorescence of Plexiglas."

The gallery also gives pretty amusing opening parties, sometimes with rock bands, which attract the hip and the staid alike, from artists to media, museum people, and collectors.

PAT HEARN

530 WEST 22ND STREET,

BETWEEN TENTH AND ELEVENTH AVENUES
(212) 727-7366
TUESDAY THROUGH SATURDAY,
11 A.M. TO 6 P.M.

Since her beginnings in 1983 in the East Village, the dealer Pat Hearn has been an art-world favorite. She has shown and promoted a strong and diverse group of artists, many women among them. Still with the gallery are such mid-career figures as the exciting abstract painter Mary Heilmann, whose canvases, in bright and inventive color combinations, do that rare thing: appeal to the senses as much as to the intellect and imagination.

Joan Jonas, who has been applying her mind and talents to almost every genre that has come to call itself art since the 1960s, shows here, too. A sculptor and painter at the start and then a pioneer in dance and movement, video, photography, and installation art, Jonas has managed to combine the genres to fascinating effect. In one of her videos, for example, performers are choreographed to walk around a downtown park holding poles, with which they create different geometric figurations and thereby redefine the landscape as they move. She also makes drawings of dogs' faces.

A lot of young artists today have been working with warm, soft, shiny colors and squishy new forms that seem to have generated a new abstract vocabulary. Here you can see some of these works in the art of Jeff

Elrod. His superflat paintings originate from drawings made with a computer-graphics program: He projects them onto canvas, marks them with masking tape, and then rolls layers of acrylic paint across the surface, all the while retaining in some jittery marks a charming suggestion of human gesture. Lisa Ruyter, who was shown in tandem with Elrod, uses her own photographs as a starting point for paintings and constructions. She takes more figurative, suburban-type imagery as a suggestive base and, using the elements out of context, creates a sense of subtle unease. Tree branches, in one work, are painted camouflage style, and the flat shape of a simple house is outlined in cheery yellow. Even Sears aluminum siding makes it onto a canvas.

The gallery celebrates time-honored pure avant-gardism in the combo of the often cartoonish, symbolic-narrative painter George Condo and the late inflammatory writer, painter, and shotgun artist William Burroughs. Condo and Burroughs actually committed their acts of painting on the same canvas, between 1988 and 1996 at Burroughs's home in Lawrence, Kansas. Condo wrote, "We both disintegrated in each other's presence and became a third being. That's who made these paintings, a third being." Well, that is sort of true: Condo did the cartoon and art-historical stuff, while Burroughs took over wherever shooting through paint cans and doors and canvas was concerned. But in the end, it's just the two of them and the way they managed to smudge boundaries.

JUNE KELLY

591 BROADWAY, 3RD FLOOR,

BETWEEN PRINCE AND HOUSTON STREETS

(212) 226-1660

TUESDAY THROUGH SATURDAY,

11 A.M. TO 6 P.M.

June Kelly has, since opening her gallery in 1986, been a staunch supporter of solid, straightforward abstract and figurative painting, sculpture, and photography by artists encompassing a wide spectrum of national, cultural, and racial origins.

African American artist Philemona Williamson, for example, paints enormous little girls engaged in ungainly and seemingly humiliating play, tumbling about with their panties showing. They appear as if they might leap right out at the viewer. Candida Alvarez, a New York artist of Puerto Rican descent, by contrast, shows paintings, collages, and drawings that also document childhood, but she embeds vaguely decipherable objects and figures in her largely abstract canvases, conjuring up her memories and dreams and exploring cultural myths.

Complicated flirtations with abstraction characterize the work of many of the gallery's artists. Kay WalkingStick, for instance, has done both abstract and representational work, seeming to gouge her images into her canvases. She recently showed charcoal drawings inspired by a sojourn in Rome.

Assemblages by Debra Priestly contain all manner of personal and symbolic objects, such as Mason jars filled with woven human hair, sweet pickles, and colored water, and others are imprinted with digitized images of family members.

ABSTRACT AND FIGURATIVE PAINTING, SCULPTURE, AND PHOTOGRAPHY

Kelly also represents the estate of Romare Bearden, whose vivid mosaics and paintings bridge the worlds of abstract art, jazz, and storytelling, along with established artists as the sculptor Elizabeth Catlett, known for her portrait heads, and the octogenarian African American painter Hughie-Lee Smith, whose WPA-inspired paintings express his social concerns, often with an added touch of surrealism.

The June Kelly gallery is located in the same building as the constantly self-renewing New Museum of Contemporary Art, on Broadway between Houston and Prince streets. From the elevator, the gallery is a small trip down the hall into a simple rectangular space, where Kelly hangs the current exhibition. But the real show is in the large back room that houses an office, storage space, archives, and a comfortable area for private viewings. And there's a lot to see here, such as some subtly colored abstract geometric canvases by the late Larry Potter, an African American expatriate who set up shop in Paris, where he was warmly welcomed in the 1960s and was deeply influenced by the jazz scene around him. His work was rediscovered in 1991 in a Paris basement, where it had sat for 25 years.

SEAN KELLY

43 MERCER STREET,

BETWEEN GRAND AND BROOME STREETS

(212) 343-2405

TUESDAY THROUGH SATURDAY,

11 A.M. TO 6 P.M.

In the four years of its existence, the Sean Kelly gallery has assembled one of the most Venice Biennale–winning groups of artists in New York. The renowned conceptualist Ann Hamilton, for instance, the United States's 1999 representative to Venice, makes installations that deal with women's lives and women's work. For one performance-installation she sat in the gallery kneading dough. Her works, often resembling contemporary renditions of Dutch still lifes, embrace sights, sounds, and smells.

Another conceptual artist with the gallery, who is also active on the international exhibition scene is Marina Abramovic. Her performances have involved a whole range of activities, from cleaning the gallery while naked to walking across the Great Wall of China and meeting her lover in the middle. That performance was not shown at the gallery.

This stark, garagelike lower-SoHo space provides an unobtrusive backdrop for a mélange of work. The most widely shown and exported Portuguese artist, the painter and sculptor Julião Sarmento, represented his country at the 1997 Venice Biennale with his characteristic depictions of women, sans heads, in casual, tentative postures, as if they were living statues. These modern-day Venuses wear garments with slits in them, suggesting violence, sexuality, and even fashion. Other Sarmento works show parts of the body in mid-gesture: a hand with a knife, a forearm with hand extended in a supplicating manner. The images all look like remnants of ancient frescoes.

The celebrated African American artist Lorna Simpson, whose large conceptual photographs sometimes deal with issues of race, also exhibits here. Her panels showing the backs of women's heads, emphasizing the quality of their hair, address the personal and social meaning of hair type, whereas her depictions of buildings and interiors (bedrooms, for example), often shown in serial images, have a cinematic quality that encourages viewers to interject a narrative.

Seriousness of a more European style comes from the Belgian videoartist and filmmaker Chantal Ackerman. Exhibiting internationally in museums and galleries, Ackerman creates stunning, compelling, and ultimately unsettling portrayals of ordinary citizens—waiting in terminals or on streets—in slow motion and with shifting focus. Little happens, but the tension increases and the viewer is inevitably drawn in. One Ackerman work documents a prostitute's day as she talks and sits at her dressing table, shops, and engages in the usual, banal activities of life.

Most media are represented here, from painting, installation, and performance to photography and video. This is an excellent place to sample many kinds of serious art today.

Phyllis Kind

136 Greene Street,

between Houston and Prince streets

(212) 925-1200

Tuesday through Saturday,

10 A.M. to 6 P.M.

There's sometimes a sense of theater at this 30-something-year-old gallery, which has always favored the rare and idiosyncratic over the trendy. Nevertheless, the art you'll see here can be very much of this moment, though it has some gnarled roots in various traditions. Among the works are witty, grotesque portrait faces by the painter Jim Nutt—so distinctive as to be characters in an allegory of his own creation—and the storytelling paintings of African American artists Robert Colescott and Roger Brown, in primary colors and frequently with social and political implications.

In fact, what most of the artworks here have in common is that they tend to be figurative and have emerged directly from the imagination, not from a model. There is the influential African American sculptor Alison Saar, who combines media, as in her tin, wire, acrylic, and enamel work *The Prize Fight,* showing two black portraits—a Madonna and Child, perhaps—in a frame adorned with squiggly, worm or thornlike shapes. The Russian artist Eric Bulatov's bright-colored, neo-Pop (or *Sots,* in Russian) canvases satirize Soviet realities.

Phyllis Kind also focuses on that currently hot genre called outsider art—that is, art by untrained people, or those with mental disorders, or even obsessives. Martin

Ramirez, for example, was a Mexican worker who lived in an asylum and painted compulsively detailed, fairy-tale-like works. One painting of a church with a small robed figure in it looks like a medieval or Persian illustration—or both. Outsider art is much like folk art and speaks of dreams, of spiritualism, and, happily for us, of eccentricity.

CONTEMPORARY AMERICAN AND EUROPEAN PAINTINGS, SCULPTURE, AND WORKS ON PAPER, INCLUDING 20TH CENTURY ART BRUT

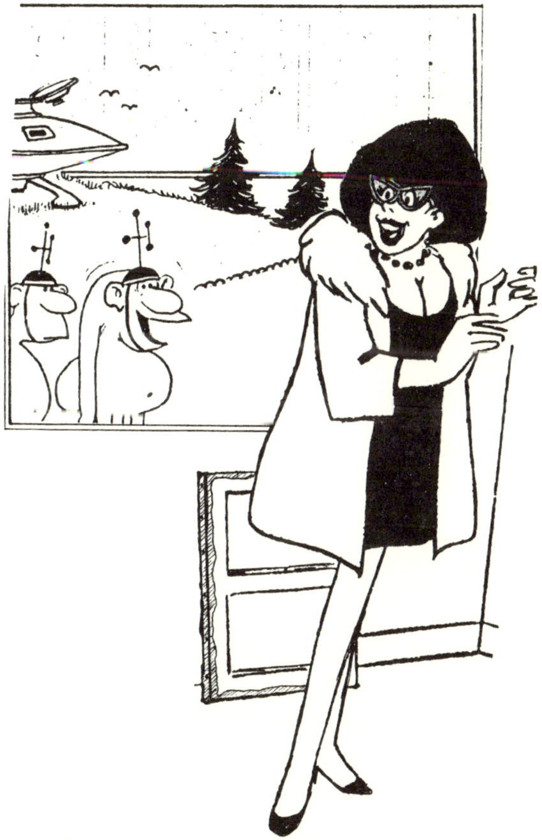

KNOEDLER & COMPANY

19 EAST 70TH STREET,

BETWEEN MADISON AND FIFTH AVENUES

(212) 794-0550

TUESDAY THROUGH FRIDAY, 9:30 A.M. TO 5:30 P.M.;

SATURDAY, 10 A.M. TO 5:30 P.M.

Despite reports to the contrary in recent years, Knoedler has insistently proved that painting—and, even more to the point, abstract painting—is not dead. Some of the genre's most popular examples can be found at this gallery, which in its 150 years has shown a single-minded dedication to abstraction in many media.

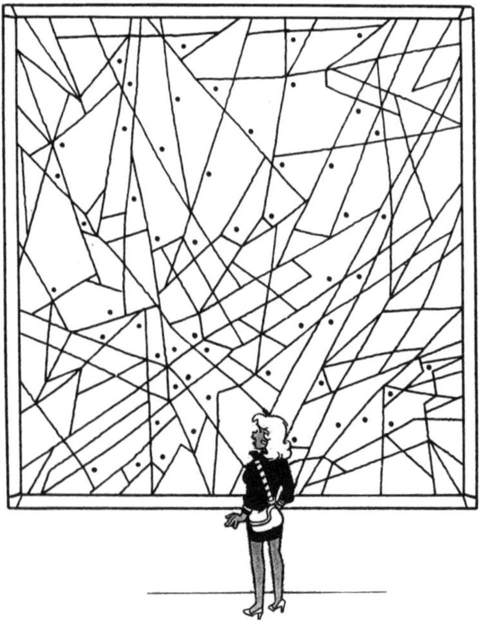

Here is work that is generally serious, finely crafted, and, for the most part, missing the proverbial "edge."

The gallery, in a stately Upper East Side town house with winding staircases and plasterwork on the ceilings, has maintained long relationships with some of the artists it represents. One of these artists is John Walker, an Englishman who works in the European tradition, blending abstraction and figuration in paintings with the expressionist overtones of the CoBrA school artists, who let the monsters of their imagination live and hide in their abstractions.

Walker's work has, however, a strong narrative element, whether in dark, active landscapes or in paintings and drawings depicting his father's experiences in World War II. His style contrasts sharply with that of the gallery's most legendary Abstract Expressionists—the late Robert Motherwell, whose estate the gallery represents, and Helen Frankenthaler, whose imageless, lyrical expressions in soft colors can be seen here on canvas, on paper, and in books.

Beauty is not to be scoffed at here. Donald Sultan, who has worked in many media over the years, even designing a deck of Minimalist playing cards, often reveals his facility with aesthetic seduction, painting enormous, blown-up fruits and flowers in layers of rich color. The works look like Andy Warhol's silk screens, enriched with cream and butter.

Anther approach to abstraction is that of the Uruguayan-born, Italy- and New York-based artist Caio Fonseca, who also flirts continually with beauty, serving up collage-like paintings in such colors as pale yellow with black, creating a pattern of personal geometry. These evoke hieroglyphs or Inca markings.

Knoedler sometimes collaborates with other galleries and institutions, exhibiting, for example, the relentlessly and playfully countercultural (any culture) former East German artist Sigmar Polke in conjunction with the Michael Werner gallery and the Museum of Modern Art, or showcasing, again with Werner, the Danish artist Per Kirkeby's stunningly rich abstract paintings that suggest intense, close-up views of woods and streams. Knoedler has also been involved in producing editions of prints and artists' books, which it often exhibits in the downstairs gallery.

While you're in the neighborhood, stop next door at the venerable Hirschl & Adler gallery, which offers a good sampling of 19th- and early-20th-century British (especially) and European art and, upstairs, at Hirschl & Adler Modern, contemporary works by the likes of Cy Twombly and Sally Apfelbaum. But whatever you do, don't forget to visit the Frick Collection, just down the block, to gain a bit of perspective on the contemporary scene.

Lehmann Maupin

Contemporary art in all media, including video and film

39 Greene Street,

between Broome and Grand streets

(212) 965-0753

Tuesday through Saturday,

10 a.m. to 6 p.m.

Owned by Rachel Lehmann, who has a gallery in Lausanne, Switzerland, and David Maupin, who was formerly the director of Metro Pictures, Lehmann Maupin, established in 1996, sports a split European-American profile. Which doesn't mean you won't also find Chinese or Indian art here.

Even the gallery space itself—SoHo grand, not slick but sophisticated—mixes New York–style industrial with European minimal in the restrained design of Dutch architect Rem Koolhaas. His signatures here: a sliding gallery wall and a greenhouse-like rear area.

What you're likely to see is not necessarily predictable. One reason is that the gallery operates as something of a *Kunsthalle*—that is, a forum for curated, thematic shows featuring work by a variety of artists not always affiliated with the gallery. Lehmann Maupin also shows artists in conjunction with other galleries, which gives it a very broad base.

The fare can range from excitingly new to reassuringly familiar, but everything reflects the owners' varied tastes and long-standing personal relationships with artists and the art community at large. You might see the space filled with work by such classic contemporaries as the British Pop-art team Gilbert & George. Their enormous, primary-colored photographs cover entire walls with much-larger-than-life self-portraits that are at once bright and melancholy. Or, in a decidedly non-Pop vein, there might be a show of the rich and moody, patterned canvases of Ross Bleckner or the postmodern pastiche paintings of David Salle, replete with classical imagery, Hollywood scenes and scenarios, and suburban tableaus. These last two eighties stars have settled into nineties maturity.

Speaking what would seem another language are the videos and installations by the British naughty girl Tracey Emin, who seems to want to shock with her deeply confessional installations tracking her love life and humiliations. One installation consists of a talky, tell-all video and a re-creation of the beach shed in which she shared her love; a rumpled bed; and then exquisite small, lyrical watercolors, mostly of herself, nearly abstract. The Swiss video artist Marie José Burki fills the gallery with large projections not of herself but of prostitutes in Belgium sitting in a window, deeply bored and distracted, waiting for clients. The very ordinariness of their responses and the seeming banality of their professional duties, conveys a poignancy that elicits empathy rather than disdain.

Come the holiday season, the gallery assembles a variety of gift-saving possibilities. In the past, they have included sculptures by the London–based Anish Kapoor. Relatively small, sinfully-rich colored, powdery-finished pieces were available at prices beginning at $7500.

Galerie Lelong

20 West 57th Street, 5th floor,

between Fifth and Sixth avenues

(212) 315-0470

Tuesday through Saturday,

10 A.M. to 5:30 P.M.

Contemporary and modern art from the United States, Europe, and Latin America

French-born and still connected to its roots, this New York branch of the Paris gallery opened in 1978. While it shows some of the same artists as the French space, like Pierre Alechinsky, a longtime champion of European figurative abstraction, the gallery has more of a diverse, New York profile.

Director Mary Sabbatino has maintained its quiet, European demeanor where gently avant-garde, international artists—including many Americans and Latin

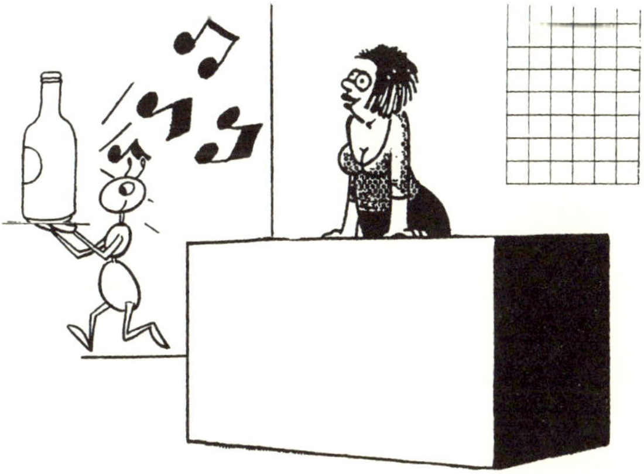

Americans, working in media from painting to sculpture to conceptual installations—exhibit. You might encounter work by the Brazilian artist Cildo Meireles, who on one occasion presented an otherworldly (and potentially volatile) installation consisting of a roomful of talcum powder, and candles for illumination; visitors removed their shoes to slog through this soft, eerie, moonlike landscape.

Another Brazilian here is Waltercio Caldas, a sculptor whose refined, Minimalist sculptures allude on the one hand to the European modernists and on the other to Brazilian architecture, concrete poetry (where the configuration of words form an image of the content), physics, and philosophy. Most of his sculptures are strict abstractions, made of metal tubing and sometimes glass, that carve up and reconfigure space.

Then there are the British, like Sean Scully, the very popular, New York–based painter, whose color combinations and stripes and bands recall many art-historical strains, from Renaissance tableaus to traditional African fabrics. Another British artist is Andy Goldsworthy, who piles up stones and other bits of nature—forming circles or walls with personal and symbolic meaning—inside the gallery as well as outdoors. He may then photograph these compositions, so that the installation and his portrayal of it constitute two different kinds of artworks, examining a subject from different perspectives.

Sculpture does seem to dominate at Lelong, as at few other New York galleries. Three important women sculptors can be seen here: the Americans Ursula von Rydingsvard and Petah Coyne and the late Cuban-born feminist Ana Mendieta, who made outdoor installations of carved and molded sand and mud—and photographed them. Her images hark back to prehistory and traditional fertility figures. Von Rydingsvard's assertive, roughly carved wood structures also look back and away from contemporary society. Some of her works resemble totem poles or primitive implements, elements drawn from nature and inspired by natural-history museums. Coyne's work, which has long taken its inspiration from nature (wire pod shapes with dark, powder-covered balls attached), from fantasy, myth, and literature (heavy wax chandelier-like sculptures hung as if in a forest, sometimes filled with candles), and from religion and fairy tales (black horsehair forms making mounds that the artist calls her little madonnas and spiderweb-like structures on the walls with stuffed animals poking out).

Lelong offers a cross-section of work by a group of mid-career artists of considerable polish and proven staying power.

Luhring Augustine

531 West 24th Street,

Between Tenth and Eleventh avenues

(212) 206-9100

Tuesday through Saturday,

10 A.M. to 6 P.M.

In the 15 years or so of its existence, Luhring Augustine has assembled a particularly wide range of strong artists, some provacative, others simply talented, some tasteful, others occasionally offensive. Its stable includes both the young and the established working in Europe, Japan, and the United States.

The British multi-prize-winning sculptor and conceptual artist Rachel Whiteread makes castings in plaster and resin of things as well as their absences—beds, bathtubs, the space beneath a chair, a resin water tower atop a building where a real one would be. More likely to offend are Larry Clark's videos and photographs of Texas teenagers doing and saying many things they shouldn't be doing or saying and Paul McCarthy's large-as-life (and even larger) mechanized installations of cowboys and other characters in cabins, also showing and doing things you wouldn't expect to see in a gallery.

One of the most engaging stars of new media showing here is the popular Swiss video artist Pipilotti Rist, who turns a playful and sometimes critical eye—with the help of seductive pop music—on society and the individual psyche. In one work, a carefree young woman strolls down the street swinging a baton, when, whoops, she suddenly thrusts it through the window of a parked car, then continues on her way, cheerfully greeting a passing policewoman.

INTERNATIONAL CONTEMPORARY ART IN ALL MEDIA

Painting, too, is alive and prospering at Luhring Augustine, including abstraction in both hot and cool guises. There are the spare, often musty green and black rectangles of Swiss artist Gunther Forg, who also shows his architectural photographs at the gallery. And coming from the more expressive direction are the English artist Fiona Rae's ebullient, wildly gestural paintings in a distinctive and varied abstract vocabulary. On your gallery rounds you're likely to find numerous Rae copycats.

Just as the offerings are disparate, so the works by individual artists can be unexpected. For example, it's hard to know what materials the American sculptor and conceptual artist Janine Antoni is likely to employ in her usually satiric works dealing with women's issues. She might be working with lipstick (a vest made of red sticks, the stuff looking both pretty and aggressive), a giant block of chocolate gnawed at the corners, or industrial-metal contraptions. It's much more certain that the trendy master of staged photographs Gregory Crewdson will populate his suburban tableaus with surreally enlarged and situated insects and strange garden detritus.

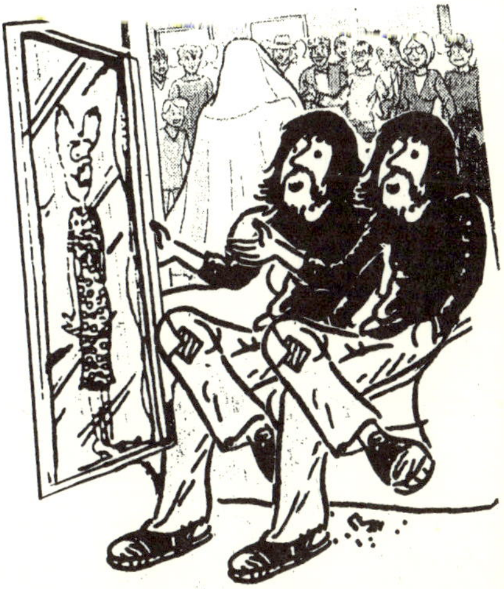

Matthew Marks

522 West 22nd Street,

between Tenth and Eleventh avenues

(212)-243-1650

Wednesday through Saturday, Noon to 6 p.m.

523 West 24th Street,

between Tenth and Eleventh avenues

(212) 243-0200

Tuesday through Saturday,

10 a.m. to 6 p.m.

Matthew Marks seems to have it all: one grand storefront midblock on 22nd Street—between the four-story Dia Center for the Arts exhibition space and the new, shop-as-ship Comme des Garçons clothing store—as well as a large, two-story venue on 24th Steet.

In his chic glass-metal-and-concrete spaces, Marks features many of the highest-profile artists working today as well as some earlier figures. Stop by either place, and you might see anything from the calligraphic works or strikingly colored abstract swirl paintings of Brice Marden to drawings and sculptures by the late Abstract Expressionist Willem de Kooning to the sculptures and paintings of the enduring (and once again hot) abstractionist Ellsworth Kelly. His vivid, garden-colored Minimalist works in shapes that have no name unexpectedly turn the gallery space into theater. (In fact, Marks says, it was Kelly who convinced him in 1993 that he should move to this then-desolate area.)

Among the newer generation represented by Marks, the young German photographer Andreas Gursky stands out. His superlarge, seemingly abstract images that look like anything but what they are—a cemetery, a supermarket shelf—are exciting to decipher.

More direct and far from ambiguous are the well-known social documentarian Nan Goldin's slick photos of teenage drug addicts: bored, perhaps naked, or just having a snack. And if that takes your appetite away, the gallery may be able to offer a stimulant: a big gingerbread house, the size of a large toolshed, by the conceptual artist Nari Ward. But you can't eat it; it's treated. Another multifaceted gallery artist is Roni Horn, who shows the most minimal of sculptures—cubes and other simple shapes in deep, jewel-toned resinous gel; bars of poetry, with lines from Emily Dickinson, strewn about and stacked; and stark, portrait photos.

Twenty-second Street was one of the first Chelsea streets to be developed for art, and it now features a string of important galleries and—still rare for the neighborhood—a shop or two and places to pause for a snack. You can and should dip into Dia and take the elevator to the roof café, or visit the real Japanese tea shop, Wild Lily, on the northern side of the block closer to Tenth Avenue. The Empire Diner, however, just across Tenth, is the place to go for bigger meals and major people-watching.

MARLBOROUGH

40 WEST 57TH STREET,

BETWEEN FIFTH AND SIXTH AVENUES

(212) 541-4900

MONDAY THROUGH FRIDAY, 10 A.M. TO 5:30 P.M.;

SATURDAY, 10 A.M. TO 5 P.M.

MARLBOROUGH CHELSEA

211 WEST 19TH STREET,

BETWEEN SEVENTH AND EIGHTH AVENUES

(212) 463-8634

MONDAY THROUGH FRIDAY, 10 A.M. TO 5:30 P.M.

One of the largest, most established, and most corporate galleries, with branches in Europe and Latin America, Marlborough has been a New York institution since 1963. The original gallery is in London. Marlborough sticks with known quantities—established artists working in traditional media. That means painting, sculpture, and works on paper by artists who tend to favor the real world. Although Marlborough used to be known for some of the prominent abstract painters it represented, not the least of them Mark Rothko and the British artist Victor Pasmore, today its focus seems to have narrowed. This is in part because the gallery now has another space in Chelsea, where it exhibits photography, abstract art, and less conventional work.

At this massive second-floor space with many exhibition areas, a sculpture garden, offices, and private viewing rooms, you might see the sensitive, psychological portrayals of people and objects in paintings by the Israeli artist Avigdor Arikha. One picture presents a man's hulking, rounded, hairy back filling the whole canvas and creating an abstract map. Another image is of a typewriter as subject and character. Speaking more boldly is the grand triumvirate of Larry Rivers, Fernando Botero, and Red Grooms, all of whom engage in exaggeration. Rivers gained his reputation with the sixties Pop artists, painting narrative scenes and portraits with old-fashioned skill and a finely honed satirical brush. Master of the partial smudge and of images designed to shock—his mother naked in a messy room; a Rembrandt scene recreated on a cigar box—Rivers maintains his sharp edge and sense of fun. Now he often works on Foamboard, carving it up for three-dimensional effect, with some homages to Hollywood's best in the mix. The Colombian artist Botero sculpts and paints his figures—provincial townsfolk and animals—to look as if they were helium filled. Their rounded and grandly overproportioned shapes are Botero's trademark, and Marlborough's own ample dimensions, particularly its sculpture garden, offer a fitting environment for them.

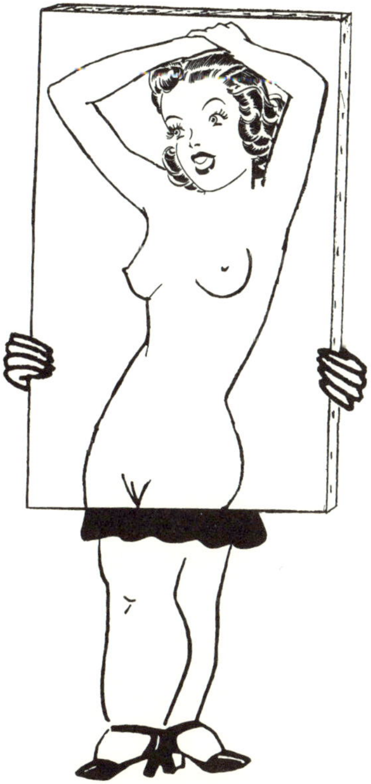

Grooms also sculpts and paints a universe of his own, with familiar caricatures of generally streetwise city types bustling their way across rickety bridges onto a Grooms-made ferry boat or into a subway car. Visitors, too, can cross the bridge, hop on the boat, and grab a seat. The artist's famous *Rumpus New York*—a miniature city in boisterous primary colors—occasionally goes on view here.

The works of two women, the Polish sculptor Magdalena Abakanowicz and the Portuguese figurative painter Paula Rego, also tend toward the outsize. Abakanowicz's large, symbolic sculptures of animals and human torsos—made in metals and strawlike materials and appearing in groups—speak clearly to political oppression. They are very assertive. So are Rego's big girls in scenes from grotesque fairy-tales.

Among the best-known Marlborough artists is the early Pop-art star Alex Katz, who continues to paint portraits of his social milieu and family in a stylized world devoid of details. In recent paintings he has also done close-up views of a small section of an apartment building or the leaves high up on a tree.

One of the best things about this gallery is the large number of prints and drawings available in all price ranges and the willingness of the staff to help you.

Mary-Anne Martin Fine Art

23 East 73rd Street,

between Madison and Fifth avenues

(212) 288-2213

Tuesday through Saturday,

11 a.m. to 5 p.m.

Latin American masters; modern and contemporary Mexican and Latin American art

One of New York's principal galleries specializing in Latin American art, both classic modern and contemporary, Mary-Anne Martin Fine Art handles artists ranging from Diego Rivera and Rufino Tamayo to Roberto Matta, Elena Climent, Gunther Gerzso, Luis Cruz Azaceta, and Alfredo Casteñeda. Even the newest work still often looks to a strong Latin American tradition of Surrealism. On the third floor of a town house—above the Kouros Gallery, known for its focus on contemporary sculpture—Martin holds exhibitions in two intimate, carpeted, and unassuming (by today's downtown standards) rooms and on the landing between them

Gallery personnel are nonintrusive yet helpful, which matters here, because what you'll see often has a colorful history. Much of the art—the Tamayos, Riveras, Wifredo Lams, and Frida Kahlos, for instance—is in the secondary-sale market, which means that the gallery buys work to sell and accepts pieces on consignment. It also provides services ranging from appraisals to advice on care and restoration and even bidding for clients at auction. At the same time, it sells new and original art.

Among recent exhibitions of living artists have been those of the work of Casteñeda, a Mexican-born painter whose stylized, Surrealistic figurative paintings recall the work of European artists of the 1930s, like Man Ray. In one image, characteristically flat and graphic, the back of a seated nude woman, looking much like a violin, is embraced by a man, his head bent at an impossible right angle, onto her shoulder; shadows (if that's what they are) on either side of the woman reiterate the shape of her buttocks. What makes Casteñeda contemporary is the degree to which his work is self-referential. The title of one exhibition is "Our I and My We."

Cruz Azaceta's work is more agitated and expressive. The Cuban artist uses a rich palette and a forceful brush along with traditional symbols to create his powerful paintings.

For those interested in Latin American culture, this gallery is something of a center. A desk in the front room holds notices and brochures about events, ranging from auctions and fairs to concerts and poetry readings.

McKee

745 Fifth Avenue,
between 57th and 58th streets
(212) 688-5951
Tuesday through Saturday,
10 A.M. to 6 P.M.

Painting, drawing, sculpture, and prints

This generously proportioned, uncluttered gallery in the Art Deco building that also houses the Mary Boone and Forum galleries is a stronghold for sculpture—there aren't too many such spaces—and for finely crafted, mostly abstract, paintings

You may have to push your way through the big crowds of tourists pouring in and out of the Warner Brothers store on the corner of 57th Street and the thinner

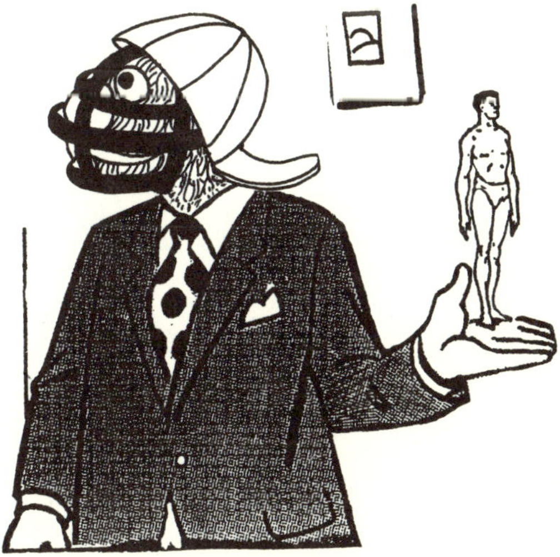

stream of shoppers flowing out of Bergdorf Goodman's men's store just to the north, but when you enter this building, the quiet seems overwhelming. The stylish lobby suggests a thirties' movie set.

Among the sculptors who show here are the American Martin Puryear, with his painstakingly fashioned, unidentifiable forms in various natural materials, and the Spaniard Susana Solano, whose strong openwork metal sculptures, clean-lined and cagelike, could be viewed as nonreferential objects or as reflections on social, religious, or political confinement.

William Tucker is another important sculptor represented by McKee. Made most frequently of wood, his straightforward, unfrilly works resemble natural forms—boulders, trees, rocks—and primal shapes. They seem at once monolithic yet warm and approachable.

The painter Vija Celmins, with her delicate conceptions of what usually look like stars in the night sky, exhibits works that are so intricately made that they seem to be more about painting itself than about any subject to which they might allude.

A real treat here is the work of the late Philip Guston (the gallery represents his estate). Guston seems increasingly to be an artist's artist, his influence showing up everywhere in the work of abstract and figurative artists today. What they take from Guston are often the details—the building-block style, the hooded Ku Klux Klan figures, or the painted stitches that remind us to read between the lines—and the composition.

Then there are the works of two dedicated mid-career painters, Jake Berthot and Harvey Quaytman, who present two well-investigated approaches to abstraction. Berthot uses expressive brushstrokes in a range of generally darkened colors and often constrains them in one rounded shape—a head, a sperm, a pod? He also tackles nature and art history, with takeoffs on van Gogh and Cézanne that seem to deconstruct those masters and emphasize the abstract nature of their apparent representation.

Quaytman a wonderful colorist, sticks to pure geometry in Minimalist compositions. Unlike many younger painters today, who are concerned with painting particularly as it relates to its physical and cultural context, Quaytman is devoted to the work itself, highlighting its materials and structure.

The sculptures of Daisy Youngblood are another matter; they might give you something of a start. Her heads of animals and humans, however artfully contorted, and close-to-life-size bronzes (of a gorilla, for one) can be playful or frightening in their intensity.

Metro Pictures

519 West 24th Street,

Between Tenth and Eleventh Avenues

(212) 206-7100

Tuesday through Saturday,

10 A.M. to 6 P.M.

Metro Pictures is a lively place, focusing on a group of mid-career artists who work in many media and seemingly have little in common. But when the gallery put together a group show of drawings by its artists, it became clear how much many of them share. A love of narrative and parody seems to prevail, and with it a certain bookishness, even if that means comic books and cartoons.

The painter Carroll Dunham, for example, shows acid-colored, sexually pugnacious paintings that feature voracious cartoon faces and a bunch of body parts out on their own doing silly things, as well as haunted houses with crazy inmates bursting out windows.

Dunham's wife, Laurie Simmons, long with the gallery, stages compositions and photographs them. She resuscitated the ventriloquist's sinister dummy Charlie McCarthy as her subject. Simmons also captures the suburban-home interiors that she composes with dollhouse furnishings, exploring childhood and nostalgia.

Cindy Sherman is one of the most in-the-news artists in the gallery, showing photographic images, based on movies and paintings of different periods, in which she often substitutes her own image for the original as a way of examining self-identity and role playing. Her photos of broken-up dolls in a baroque-looking stew of rotting vegetables are chilling evocations of subconscious fears and nightmares.

Another artist conducting some bizarre psychological investigations here is Tony Oursler, who makes installations with videotaped faces stuck among props and disembodied voices complaining to the viewer. Sometimes you'll find, hidden amid foliage or under blankets, images of eyes blinking or mouths moving.

Mike Kelley does many things. Among them he parodies old-fashioned paperback-book covers and sticks them in revolving racks, devises illustrated stories, and makes mysterious landscapes in vitrines. And Gary Simmons shows large, chalkboard-like black-and-white paintings that look like real blackboard erasures but are are actually smears of white paint.

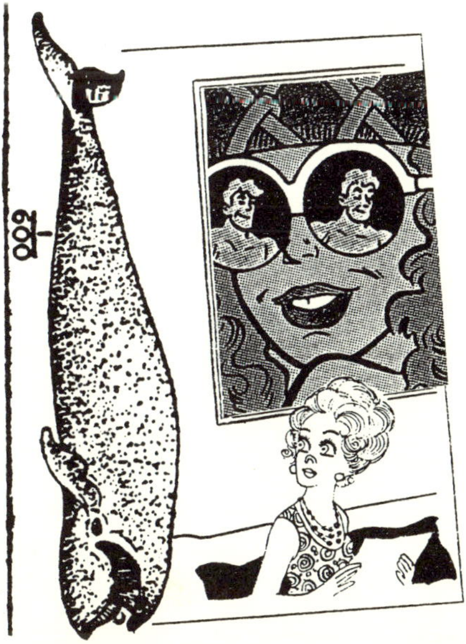

Nolan/Eckman

560 Broadway, 6th floor,
at Prince Street
(212) 925-6190
Tuesday through Friday, 10 a.m. to 6 p.m.;
Saturday, 11 a.m. to 6 p.m.

Showing mostly works on paper by established, mid-career artists from Europe and the United States, Nolan/Eckman focuses on the intellectual and emotional underpinnings of many important artists today. Representing the avant-garde of this moment as well as slightly earlier artists of this century, the gallery's focus leans toward the cerebral. That means some conceptual work by the British artist Ian Hamilton Finlay, who shows enigmatic, formal installations addressing such subjects as history, art history, and formal gardens; and stark, deadpan Cibachrome portraits by German artist Rosemarie Trockel. It has also included the disturbing work of German artist Hermann Nitsch, who sometimes uses blood as a painterly medium, often from slaughtered animals that he photographs and draws.

The exhibitions at this moderate-size gallery, above Dean & DeLuca's fabled gourmet emporium, tend to be filled with smallish works that can be emotionally intense and very funny. Witness the New York artist Carroll Dunham's hilarious drawings, not unlike his paintings but smaller and more concentrated and missing the cacophony of clashing, acidic colors. Dunham's recurring cartoonish character appears whole or in parts—sometimes as lips and big teeth or as penises assuming the posture of guns. It's certainly a topsy-turvy world.

New York sculptor Barry Le Va shows his drawings here, which sometimes look like blueprints (really blackprints) for his sculptural installations—geometrically shaped boulders that reconfigure interior and exterior landscapes.

CONTEMPORARY AMERICAN AND EUROPEAN WORKS ON PAPER IN ALL MEDIA

The gallery also features some expressive Europeans. One of them is the German virtuoso of both abstraction and figuration, in paint and photography, Gerhard Richter. Richter's precise and affecting landscapes, his famous, influential way of scraping surfaces to expose many-colored layers of paint in one gesture, as well as the paintings that look like blurred photos, demonstrate just a few of the tricks in his repertoire. The former East German artist Sigmar Polke brings his high-art, low-art nonart sensibility to the gallery in quick line drawings that can be satiric or artful.

Another versatile figure is the late German artist Martin Kippenberger who could be very funny, following his absurd thoughts any which way and in any form. An installation right after his death, in 1997, presented a meditation on cigarettes, involving sculpture, objects in vitrines, drawings, and more. Absurdity and stream of consciousness are at the heart of his humor.

William Copley, an American and a gallery regular, specializes in sharply satiric narratives in black ink on paper, reminiscent of comics and George Grosz. Content is still in fashion at Nolan/Eckman.

PaceWildenstein

142 Greene Street,

between Houston and Prince streets

(212) 431-9224

Tuesday through Saturday, 10 A.M. to 6 P.M.

32 East 57th Street,

between Park and Madision avenues

(212) 421-3292

Tuesday through Friday, 9:30 A.M. to 5:30 P.M.; Saturday, 10 A.M. to 6 P.M.

A haven for well-known, fully emerged artists at the gallery's 57th Street and SoHo locations, PaceWildenstein is almost a department store for classic, sanctified contemporary art. Come here to see the works of stars like Robert Ryman, Agnes Martin, Claes Oldenburg, Kiki Smith, Joel Shapiro, Julian Schnabel, Robert Mangold, Robert Rauschenberg, and on and on.

The octogenarian Agnes Martin's strictly Minimalist, exquisitely and subtly colored canvases, striped or finely gridded, encourage you to take long and close looks so that the tonal relations and the composition itself may "develop."

Kiki Smith shows her sometimes neo-Romantic, wistful explorations of nature and natural phenomena along with traditional and personal myths in fragile-looking drawings and collages on tissue-like paper, stuffed birds, videos of nature in action, a screen made of translucent panels dedicated to the strength of the moon, and glass birds' nests.

In these, as in the paintings of Robert Mangold, whose finely limned ellipses have long been gracing his elegantly colored and sometimes shaped canvases, drawings, prints, and wall sculptures, the tone seems relatively cool. But it all heats up in the sculptures, paintings, and photographs of Lucas Samaras, for whom materials like knives, nails (of the metal sort), and little mirrors lure, threaten, and amuse, in one look.

The bumptious paintings of Julian Schnabel sometimes feature his famed smashed plates, which create the equivalent of Abstract Expressionist painting. He also

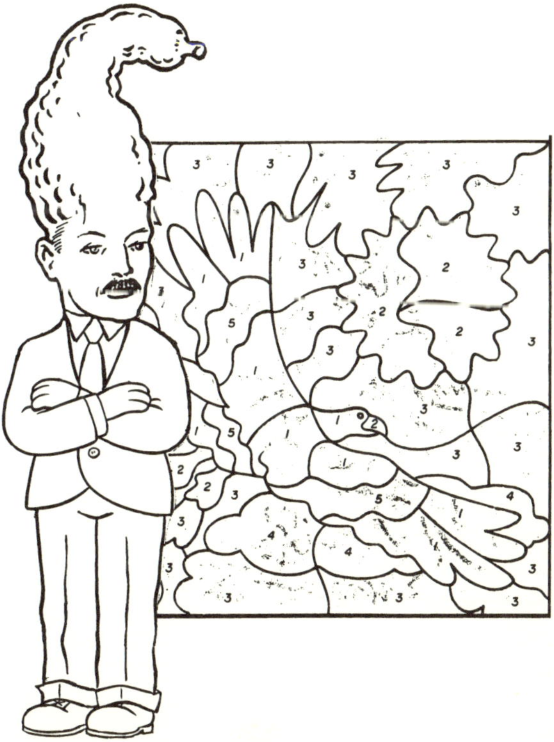

does portraits after artists like Goya with contemporary figures, including his son, as subjects. His approach to these combines traditional painting with contemporary gestures.

Joel Shapiro's almost playful sculptures—often reductions of human figures or of trees—seem to be caught in mid-motion. And the Pop-art hero Claes Oldenburg's cornucopia of oversize objects—or miniaturizations, as in his *Mouse Museum*—are always fun, however serious their underlying meaning. Oldenburg and his wife, Coosje van Bruggen, have long been collaborating on the effects of scale and material on our understanding of everyday objects, giving the objects themselves—a giant toothbrush, a jar stuffed with words, a soft saxophone—a human power and poignancy.

Although it is a barometer of the blue-chip market, PaceWildenstein is not as inaccessible as you might think in terms of content or price. If you go to the 57th Street location and climb the spiral stairs in the middle of the main gallery, you'll find a large selection of graphic work by contemporary artists as well as modern and Old Master prints for reasonable prices. And that's not all. In the same building you can visit Pace-Wildenstein Macgill, which specializes in 20th-century photography, and Pace Primitives, which features African art.

POSTMASTERS

459 WEST 19TH STREET,
BETWEEN NINTH AND TENTH AVENUES
(212) 727-3323
TUESDAY THROUGH SATURDAY,
11 A.M. TO 6 P.M.

CONTEMPORARY PAINTING, SCULPTURE, PHOTOGRAPHS

In a beautiful Chelsea ground-floor location with frosted-glass doors and two large, well-proportioned viewing areas, this sophisticated gallery covers a broad swath of artists and attracts a spectrum of fans. A show of allover abstract-cartoon paintings by Christian Schumann invites viewers to find images in the brightly-colored melange. They'll discover furious, comic-style characters moving in a frenetic jumble of motion and pattern. A different cartoon spirit informs the paintings of Elliott Green, whose interconnected figures of real and imagined genres of animals and humans and of sexual configurations hark back to French and English satiric art of the 18th century, to dance, and to those stretched out, transmogrifying characters of movie and comic fame.

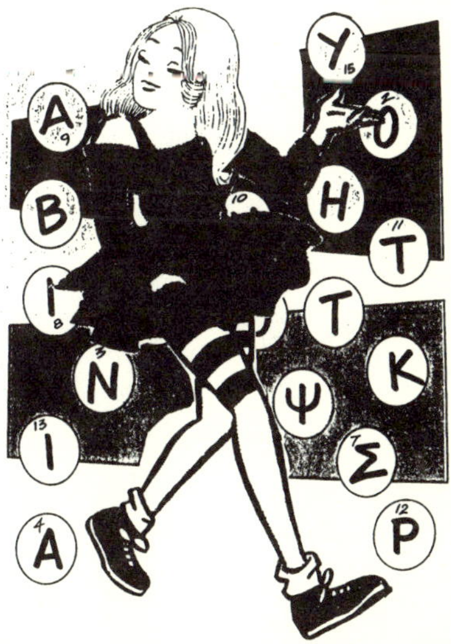

Mary Kelly is famous for another kind of art. Her *Post-Partum Document* used dirty diapers as a medium, making a kind of feminist statement, while her recent installation at Postmasters called *Mea Culpa* featured dried lint, right out of a clothes dryer. Kelly took the naturally curved sheets of lint and printed on them texts culled from media accounts of international atrocities. Hanging end to end around the room, the work looks at first like a white Minimalist piece. But up close the texts become visible, and it's apparent that the installation is about all kinds of cleansing.

Funkiness—or, better, moldiness—is the order when Ken Feingold "grows photos" by suspending negatives over paper or glass set in water where algae cultures are growing. The photographs that result, bearing the series title "Bacteria Rule," marry art with nature and a bit of high-school science project. Accident makes the final image as the algae grow their own pattern.

Spencer Finch's investigations of perception have been documented at the gallery in paintings and works on paper. The often delicate images offer no initial clue as to how they were obtained. But one installation documented a visit to Sweden, where Finch made studies of light patterns coming from different directions, capturing their "prints" in subtle, Minimalist images on photographic paper.

Postmaster's also represents the Swiss artist Sylvie Fleury, whose work in many media—recently, blow-up plastic—relates to fashion (in an ironic way, of course) with exhibition titles like "Is Your Makeup Crushproof?" The gallery's well-rounded gathering of contemporary artists also comprises solid, less flamboyant abstract painters, like Donna Moylan and David Diao.

Max Protetch

511 West 22nd Street,

between Tenth and Eleventh avenues

(212) 633-6999

Tuesday through Saturday,

10 a.m. to 6 p.m.

Contemporary painting, sculpture, ceramics, and architectural drawings

Since its establishment in 1969, Max Protetch has carved out a curious niche for itself. One of the few galleries to feature architectural projects, including drawings and models, along with art, it has on its roster the Americans Peter Eisenman and Michael Graves as well as the Japanese architect Tadao Ando and the Brazilian landscape architect Roberto Burle-Marx. One recent exhibition featured paintings, Plexiglas models, and sculptures related to the brand-new, wildly curvy and dramatic Cincinnati Contemporary Arts Center, designed by the London-based architect Zaha Hadid.

Besides the architecture-related projects, Protetch has been featuring the artworks of an international cast that includes the Beijing-based artist Zhang Huan, who makes performance art and photographs, among them images of migrant workers in a pond and nude bodies piled one atop the other. Byron Kim also works in many media: he has done paintings composed of a grid of peach beige, and tan tones representing skin colors; made an installation composed of the contents of vacuum cleaners, mixed them with a liquid, and painted walls with the substance, showing the lives of the building's inhabitants through their detritus; and took photographs of seascapes and skyscapes to document a visit to Ireland.

In a more concrete mode, gallery artists Betty Woodman and Richard DeVore work in ceramics: Woodman's are fantastic, Cubistic confections, somewhere between sculpture and pottery; DeVore makes large, black Minimalist vessels. Protetch also represents the estate of the sculptor Scott Burton, famous for his useful sculptures—Minimalist benches and tables in such materials as granite, marble, steel, and glass.

Among the major, generally mid-career artists who show here is David Reed, a much-in-the-news painter, who has expanded his repertoire to include film and props—all at once. Known for his large, ribbony, often intercepted strokes of paint (gestures evoking Pop artist Roy Lichtenstein) and serial swirls hinting at narrative lines, he has interjected his paintings into videos and movies. For instance, his installation *Scottie's Bedroom,* from Alfred Hitchcock's *Vertigo*, features a bed (reproduced from the film) with a Reed painting over it and a television playing the real scene from the movie but incorporating Reed's painting into it—over the bed, of course. Which is the real art, and where is it?

The sculptor Oliver Herring is best known for creating otherworldly figures out of knit Mylar, an alluring, transparent material suggesting, most of all, absence—of life, of color, of meaning. Sometimes he shows his figures with videos of himself engaged in repetitive actions, engaging with geometric objects.

New to this mix is the Italian *arte povera* artist Michelangelo Pistoletto, who exhibits his typically intellectual projects, including an installation of several sculptures that look like gateways at various angles and a TV screen displaying the words "Does God exist? Yes I do."

ANDREA ROSEN

525 WEST 24TH STREET,

BETWEEN TENTH AND ELEVENTH AVENUES

(212) 627-6000

TUESDAY THROUGH SATURDAY,

10 A.M. TO 6 P.M.

CONTENT-ORIENTED WORK IN ALL MEDIA

A power hitter, the dealer Andrea Rosen has successfully positioned herself at the hub of today's youngish avant-garde. The "content-oriented" work the gallery claims to focus on tends to be broadly drawn and satiric in nature. This is not a subtle space. Painter John Currin, for example, presents his composite Barbie types, of all ages, striking in their faux-realist demeanors and grotesque postures. His portrait entitled *The Cripple* shows a laughing ingenue with a wholesome face, a strikingly sexy exposed bosom, and an eye-arresting cane.

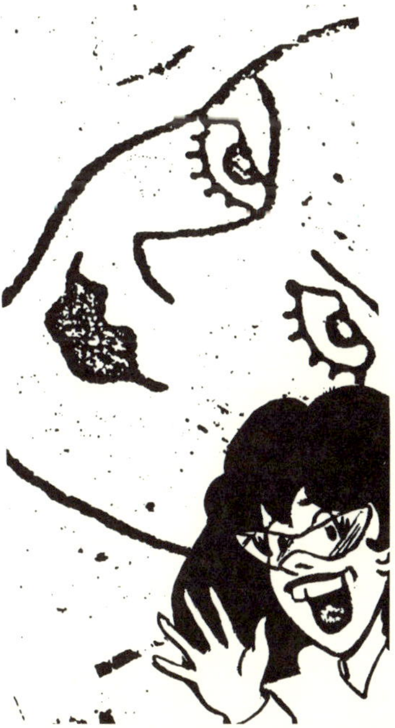

Meanwhile, Sean Landers, another satirist working in various media, takes Magrittean Surrealism into the future. In one painting a Tin-Woodsman-cum-Martian head has horns coming out the ears and three extraterrestrial rings above it. Calipers work as legs. The backdrop for it all is a handwritten diary entry in imperfect, wavy columns, oddly evoking the Cubists' collaging of objects with newspapers.

The late conceptual artist Felix Gonzalez-Torres lives on in the gallery, in his characteristic piles of posters for visitors to take away, festooned, for example, with photos of the FBI's "most wanted" or of victims. As a testimonial to transience, one of his works consisted simply of a pile of hard candy, to be replenished as eaten.

One of the gallery's most-noted artists today is Andrea Zittel, courted by international biennials and the recipient of a recent Public Art Fund commission. Zittel is concerned with making environments; these can consist of ingenious fold-up boxes for living. Calling to mind Shaker design, the Bauhaus, Frank Lloyd Wright, and Mondrian, they might feature, for example, a bed, bookshelves, and a mini-kitchen, or various other combos. Her gallery installation of large fake rocks with magazines strewn about and a television set, providing an instant leisure environment, is paralleled in her current Public Art Fund installation set in Central Park, where her homemade rocks do indeed imitate and rival nature.

This is an outspoken and inventive place and sometimes successfully shocking. Here you can see photographer John Coplans's close-ups of his aging body—all parts of it. But these images, shown in juxtaposition with one another, have an architectural and abstract quality to them and, at the same time, a poignancy.

Betsy Senior

375 West Broadway,
between Broome and Spring streets
(212) 941-0960
Tuesday through Saturday,
10 A.M. to 6 P.M.

Contemporary prints and drawing

This is a wonderful place to see experiments in printmaking as well as drawings by some of today's most serious mid-career artists. Also, Betsy Senior shares exhibition space with another strong print gallery—Gemini G.E.L. at Joni Moisant Weyl—which complements her offerings and gives visitors a two-for-one experience. Gemini shows prints by a wide cross-section of contemporary artists, while Senior tends to focus on a more specific group of mid-career artists, some not known for their works on paper.

One show featured work by the noted abstractionist Ross Bleckner, famous for his compulsively crafted, sleek-surfaced, moody paintings, but not known for his etchings, which were on view here. Similarly, Senior has shown the black-and-white etchings of Joel Shapiro, generally recognized for his animated abstract sculptures. Inspired by the print medium, he portrayed images of figures engaged in struggle. These might be read as a fleshing out of his sculpture or as an escape from them.

A number of the artists here have worked in collaboration with the painter and printmaker David Lasry, whose Two Palms press allows artists to experiment with a sculptural kind of printmaking that uses a thick, soft paper and the kind of press that was once employed to stamp rubber. Among them are David Row, who paints and prints works based on ellipses in striking color combinations; Mel Bochner, a conceptual artist who paints and draws using numerical relations on geometric grounds; Jessica Stockholder, the Abstract Expressionist working in three dimensions; and the ubiquitous Sol LeWitt, whose works of all sizes in brilliant color combinations are either done by him or made according to his plans.

This is a tasteful gallery, where the dealer's keen eye and careful attention to detail is apparent. It is also characterized by an air of unpredictability. You can find works by such a wide range of artists that it encompasses the very figurative William Bailey, the refined abstractionists Valerie Jaudon and Jacqueline Humphries, the politically and graphically dextrous Glenn Ligon, and Brazilian artist Beatriz Milhazes, who produces layers of lacy patterns translated into print.

Visit Betsy Senior not only to view the current exhibition but also for the opportunity to see what's in the drawers and racks full of works, often reasonably priced.

Tony Shafrazi

119 Wooster Street,
between Prince and Spring streets
(212) 274-9300
Tuesday through Saturday,
10 A.M. to 6 P.M.

Contemporary paintings, sculpture, works on paper, and prints

Everything at this gallery seems bold. Tony Shafrazi is not a subtle space. With a bright and cavernous main room and an exhibition area downstairs, the gallery has generous proportions and a wall of storefront windows that make it extremely accessible and often alluring. Of course, this also means you can zoom by and glimpse almost an entire show without even entering, but more often you'll be drawn in by the assertiveness, even rambunctiousness, of the works.

The strikingly graphic and weirdly playful post-graffiti art of the late Keith Haring is balanced here by the famously contorted imaginings of the late, great, debauched British painter Francis Bacon (the gallery now represents his estate). You might even be startled to discover floor-to-ceiling images of urinals—drawings and paintings—in homage to the

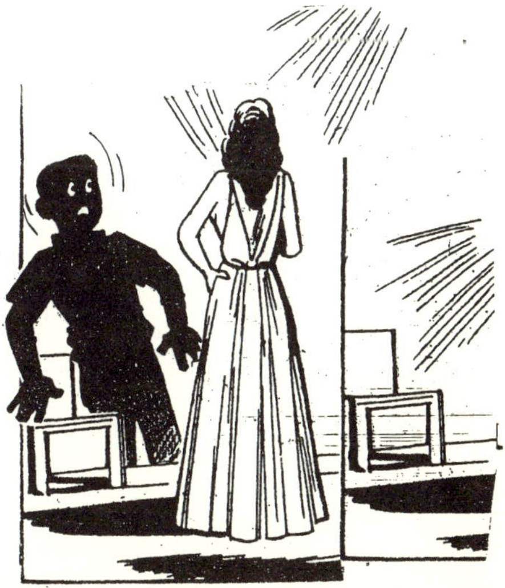

king of conceptual artists, Marcel Duchamp, by his most loyal and witty American interpreter, Mike Bidlo, whose installation assumes the guise of a hallowed cathedral.

The African American painter and collagist Michael Ray Charles's sophisticated and hilarious takes on clichés of black life and history might also draw you into the gallery. One picture, for example, parodies a coloring book with paper dolls: here a cartoonlike caricature of a black boy—with circles for eyes and for mouth—is surrounded by "accessories" to cut out, among them a gun, a football, a tie, a banana, and such.

Then there is the celebrity contingent, Hollywood's own Dennis Hopper among them. Hopper shows his film noir–ish photos and draws fellow celebs to openings.

Sometimes you might wonder where you are when you see the stained-glass installations of the British artist Brian Clarke, who creates abstract walls and screens. Is this an updated Art Nouveau restaurant, a Hollywood hotel lobby, a stage set, or a cathedral (not the same one as Bidlo's, of course)? Striking a quieter though still grand note are Donald Baechler's collage-paintings. Measuring an expansive 12 feet square, they assault the eye with their old-corner-candy-shop charm and child-like imagery. A monstrous ice-cream cone or a gloppy sundae dominating a picture may quickly yield to more subtle surrounding images—faded photographs, pictures of balls, burlap grain bags, and the personal narratives they conjure up. They hint nostalgically at the kind of objects that stimulate a boy to become an artist.

JACK SHAINMAN

513 WEST 20TH STREET,
BETWEEN TENTH AND ELEVENTH AVENUES
(212) 645-1701
TUESDAY THROUGH SATURDAY,
10 A.M. TO 6 P.M.

CONTEMPORARY SCULPTURE, PHOTOGRAPHY, PAINTING, AND VIDEO, PRIMARILY FROM EUROPE, CANADA, AND THE UNITED STATES

What you see when you enter the Jack Shainman gallery isn't all you get. The smartly designed exhibition spaces on the main level present all manner of contemporary art—from the abstract to the figurative, from sculpture to photography, video, and installations—by a lively assemblage of young-to-middling and even elderly American, Canadian, and European artists. Besides the gallery shows, there's another scene below, where a wealth of African and Indian art, gathered by the artist and gallery associate Claude Simard, is stored.

Shainman, whose first gallery was in Washington, D.C., moved to New York in 1986, opening spaces in the East Village and then SoHo before finally taking the Chelsea plunge. Proof of the gallery's popularity is the friendly set of regulars who show up at openings. It seems there is something for everyone here. You might find frescolike, close-up portraits by the German artist Till Freiwald; brilliantly strange-colored, sculpted-paint canvases by the New York artist Leslie Wayne; the narrative, sometimes politically charged paintings of the Chicago-based African American artist Kerry James Marshall; and jewel-toned, color-built paintings by Spaniard Prudencio Irazabal.

You could also see the Quebec-born Simard's own work, which enlists painting, photography, sculpture, and taxidermy to address issues of personal and national identity. It can be funny, too.

Computer-assisted art gets its due in mutant-looking photographs and sculptures by the team Aziz and Cucher. And then there's Betty Goodwin, the long-reigning Toronto priestess of many of the quiet avant-garde movements of the last half of this century. Her work, like that of Louise Bourgeois, ranges from delicate line drawings to disturbing sculptures featuring dangling body parts to Minimalist installations. Shainman is an original force on this rich block of contemporary spaces that includes the galleries in Chelsea's first "mall" building, at 529 West 20th Street, and Feigen Contemporary.

Holly Solomon

Contemporary Art in All Media

172 Mercer Street,
corner of Houston street
(212) 941-5777
Tuesday through Saturday,
10 A.M. to 6 P.M.

Holly Solomon has been energizing the art market since 1975, first in the East Village, then on 57th Street, and now in SoHo. Her multilevel space—formerly occupied by a health club—is well situated for the gallery-goer. It's down the block from some chic, yuppie-type bars and opposite the Angelika Film Center, which shows six films at a time.

Solomon continues to keep her gallery and herself high profile. She is frequently interviewed in the press and even turns up in bus, subway, and magazine ads for Coach leather products. Funky, sometimes political, and often decorative, the fare here is varied. The gallery is known for its interest in pattern painting, exemplified by some of the recent work of Julia Jacquette, who showed a nostalgic series of popular portrayals of women's faces from the 1930s, laid out in a grid. Patterns also mark the oeuvre of the gallery's most famous artist, Nam June Paik, widely held to be the progenitor of video art as we know it. His constructions—sculptures, really—composed of functioning television sets showing various images at once, document, parody, and celebrate 20th-century culture and the introduction of technology.

Among the other artists you may see here is the Conceptualist Rob Wynne, whose imaginative works touch on Surrealism, literature, history, and natural history. His shows might feature a sculpture of glass shoes or a roomful of wallpaper patterned with snakes or butterflies—conjuring up mythological and psychological associations—or needlepoint frames with woven quotations or aphoristic sayings surrounding an absurd or sexually provocative 18th-century French illustration.

Also taking off on the idea of patterning is Kim MacConnel, who compulsively collages all manner of wildly colored images and objects—notably, tiny dolls' clothes, on hangers; and little tea trays. These are like tourist tchotchkes, but from his own personal culture. Photographer Barbara Pollack does nothing similar; instead, she dickers with reality, using a Polaroid camera and, often, her family and friends as subjects. But the images are blurred closeups that barely reveal any details of the people being portrayed. They create an atmosphere in which the subjects advance and recede in the eye of the photographer. They're about what happens in the space between.

SONNABEND

420 WEST BROADWAY,
BETWEEN PRINCE AND SPRING STREETS
(212) 966-6160
TUESDAY THROUGH SATURDAY,
10 A.M. TO 6 P.M.

CONTEMPORARY AMERICAN AND EUROPEAN ART; PAINTING, SCULPTURE, AND PHOTOGRAPHY

A high-toned modern gallery with a few bolder, try-to-shock-you artists in the mix, Sonnabend has been a major player in the contemporary arena since its founding in 1971 by Ileana Sonnabend. Some of its 20 or so artists have been with the gallery since the beginning, notably the singing, painting, photographing, and what-have-you conceptual pair Gilbert & George. The British duo inaugurated their celebrated routine at the gallery that first year, painting themselves silver and gold,

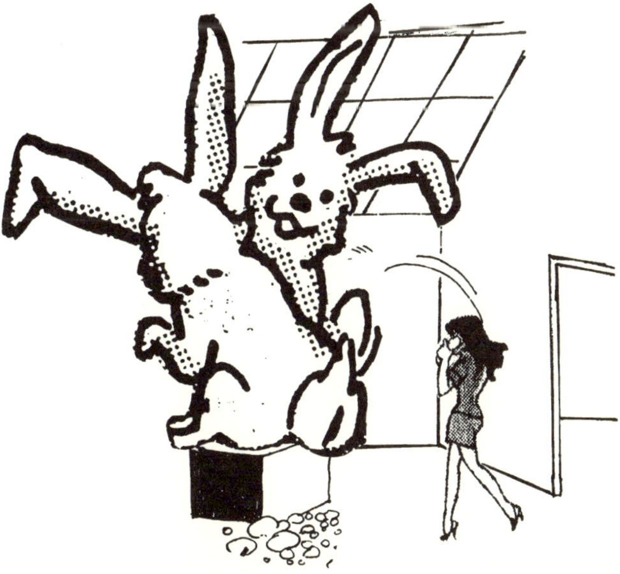

standing atop a card table, with speakers below, turning very slowly, and singing with nearly immobile faces the music-hall song "Underneath the Arches." A couple of years ago they did a repeat performance. Spanning pre-Pop and post-Pop, they have since shown their poster-colored, paneled, floor-to-ceiling paintings of themselves (as always), sometimes nude, and with such accoutrements as microscopic enlargements of bodily secretions, looking ever so pretty and abstract.

It's a far cry from there to the formal, black-and-white and stone-cold-gray photographs of industrial structures by the German couple Bernd and Hilla Becher. The strikingly repetitive images, all taken close-up against a manipulated, neutral background, have an air of melancholy about them, as well as an unanticipated grace. Sometimes the Bechers even lend their subjects a hint of human attitude as they capture them from various angles.

Japan's Hiroshi Sugimoto, who also exhibits here, makes refined photographic images of nature or architecture, but his have a softer, less defined perspective, giving the work a spiritual aura.

The gallery's stable includes such long-running, influential artists as John Baldessari, known for the solid-colored opaque dots he affixes to paintings and photographs, frustratingly obstructing our views, and the still-prevailing Pop star Robert Rauschenberg, whose "combines" (big three-dimensional collages), paintings, and prints stand as landmarks in the art history of this century. Robert Yarber is something else, with his lurid-toned nightmares (people flying off apartment balconies) and city views, played out in paintings and photos. Their shading suggests a combination of 3-D comics—before you put on the glasses—and El Greco. And conceptual artist Mel Bochner, concerned with underlying structures of meaning, might install a floor puzzle, each piece filled with a number, as in a giant hopscotch game, exploring various progressions and relations.

Coming out of a movement called Neo-Geo (which emerged as a reaction against the frenzy of Neo-Expressionism), a kind of revival of geometric abstraction, are two gallery artists whose paths have diverged. Terry Winters has taken his weblike paintings, prints, and drawings further into the realm of pure abstraction, while Ashley Bickerton has delved into very overt satire of contemporary character types: a fat New Age woman meditating, a narcissistic bodybuilder, and so on.

Showing other important artists, such as installationist Haim Steinbach, sculptor Barry Le Va, and Robert Morris, with his frightening apocolyptic visions in charred paintings and installations, the gallery offers a sophisticated sampling of contemporary art's most established movements in the late 20th century.

Sperone Westwater

142 Greene Street,

Between Prince and Houston streets

(212) 431-3685

Tuesday through Saturday,

10 A.M. to 6 P.M.

One of the most consistently interesting contemporary galleries, Sperone Westwater represents an imaginative and serious international array of artists of many persuasions. The committed painter Susan Rothenberg has long excavated nature, the psyche, and mythology in producing expressionistic, semirepresentational portrayals of human body parts, horses, and skeletons in rich desert colors, whereas her husband, Bruce Nauman, a leading Conceptualist working in many media, explores nature, human nature, chance, violence, and play, in sculpture, video, prints, performance, and painting.

Another gallery artist whose influence is pervasive among abstract painters today is Jonathan Lasker. His bright, visually witty, often primary-colored canvases consider many lines of abstract thinking at once. One of his most-quoted devices is the thick-painted scribble, like a pile of rope; it appears in most of his paintings and inevitably refers to language and thought as well as to the nature of the materials that produce it. (Spaghetti also comes to mind.)

The linear scrawl characterizes the work of other artists in the gallery, which also shows the venerable master Cy Twombly. Twombly's talkative interchanges between the wild line and the splotch have come to exemplify how abstract elements have as much communicative power as representational ones do.

The Argentine painter Guillermo Kuitca, with his intricate, painted mappings of exteriors (streets, graveyards) and interiors (rooms, libraries, opera houses, and minds), plumbs various realities, as does the Italian sculptor-painter Mimmo Paladino, whose bright-colored works are filled with myth and symbol.

You can also see the the German Conceptualist Wolfgang Laib's beeswax sculptures, such as one that resembles an Egyptian tomb, or mastaba, with steps going up one side, imbuing the gallery with an intoxicating scent. Or walk around the American sculptor Richard Tuttle's playful primary-colored paper constructions. Or wonder whether the British artist Malcolm Morley's paintings, with boats and toy warplanes sticking out of them, are longing for childhood or just very angry. But if you don't know her work already, you're likely to be the most surprised by Kim Dingle's realistic-looking, child-size dolls, in girly dresses and eyeglasses, bursting out of walls.

Sometimes the gallery steps farther afield: with a large show of Persian miniatures, for example, or an exhibition of 14th-century Italian primitive paintings juxtaposed with gold paintings marked by slits, by the late-Minimalist painter Lucio Fontana.

Staley-Wise

560 Broadway,
between Prince and Spring streets
(212) 966-6223
Tuesday through Saturday,
11 A.M. to 5 P.M.

Featuring photography done throughout the century, this gallery offers both public and intimate glimpses of the stars, the gods and goddesses of fashion—those who design it, model it, and wear it—and celebrities of every other stripe. This is generally not cutting-edge art but professional photography at its best. Among the perpetrators of these images are such luminaries as Cecil Beaton, Louise Dahl-Wolfe, Disfarmer, Horst P. Horst, George Hurrell, Andre Kertesz, Jacques-Henri Lartigue, Herbert Matter, Helmut Newton, Herb Ritts, Edward Steichen, and Bert Stern.

Worshipers of Audrey Hepburn can get their nostalgia fix when shows like "Audrey Style" offer portraits of the big-eyed goddess by 10 photographers at once, among them, Beaton, Sid Avery, and Raymond Voinquel.

The very-today photographer David LaChapelle, who takes bright and tawdry images of the glitterati (and perverts and society hangers-on) in kinky disarray, also shows here and at places like Tony Shafrazi. LaChapelle's dysfunctional, amputated society shows itself in such images as a model in a Batman cape with a peg leg and a hook for a hand. The art critic Grace

Glueck writes, "Mr. LaChapelle is the baddest boy ever. His work is cool, hip, kinky—and very icky."

TWENTIETH-CENTURY PHOTOGRAPHY INCLUDING FASHION, PORTRAITURE, STYLE, AND HOLLYWOOD PHOTOGRAPHS

But not everything here is about celebrity. Among the younger generation of photographers is the Dutch-born Ellen Von Unwerth, whose work, such as the series "Original Sin," features images of sexy young women, dressed and undressed, apparently having fun. And the New York–based Leah Demchick has captured India in vivid color.

This is a gallery where subject is still very important and where the images are elegant and forthright.

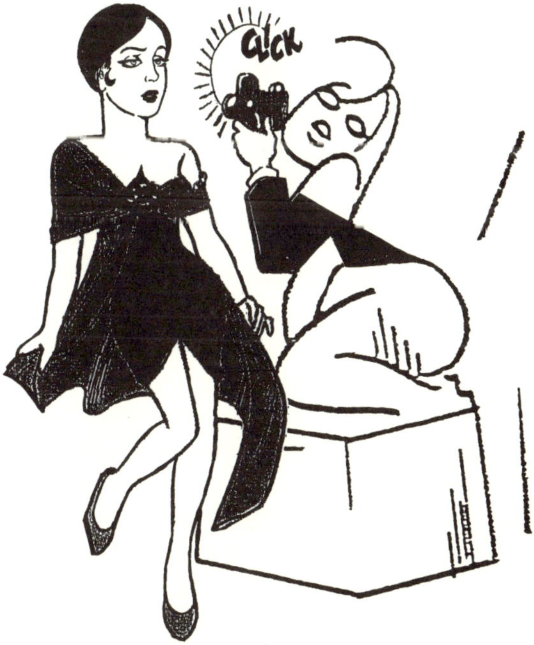

Jack Tilton

49 Greene Street,
between Broome and Grand streets
(212) 941-1775
Tuesday through Saturday,
10 A.M. to 6 P.M.

Jack Tilton shows the gamut of international art—abstract, figurative, conceptual, performance—in all media. In business since 1983, Jack Tilton, who used to work at the legendary Betty Parsons gallery, began on 57th Street before moving downtown to SoHo, where he built an international roster. Today that comprises American and European artists as well as some very inventive Chinese artists. Interestingly, the Eastern artists here are sometimes more adventuresome than the others.

As one art consultant ventured, when anything is hot, Jack Tilton is quick to know about it. You're as likely to see Nicole Eisenman's witty, often biting paintings and works in various media, packed and layered with images—stealing from life, TV, and cartoons—as you are to see the surreal installations of the Mexican artist Eduardo Abaroa, who had a show here entitled "Recent Models and Freaks." Abaroa mixes TV, toys, and plants, for example, in his stylish look at consumer and personal culture: his depiction of a flower with an eye in it and a big flayed bee (looking like a human organ) hovering close by is strikingly reminiscent of the Symbolist painter Odilon Redon's *Cyclops*.

More outrageous is the Chinese artist Xu Bing, who turned the gallery into a giant pigpen with straw and fencing and a bunch of live pigs wearing—what else?—sheep masks. By comparison, the work of the American painter Fred Tomaselli looks pretty tame. His very attractive, compulsively constructed mixed-media compositions are often made of pills, hemp, resin, and sundry oddities.

ABSTRACT PAINTING, FIGURATIVE DRAWING, CONCEPTUAL SCULPTURES, AND INSTALLATION ART

Another Chinese artist, Zhang Peili, does video projections, one of them a large, very slow-motion, blurry close-up of the top of a building with a wispy tree and a red balloon floating in front of it, pulling our eye continually upward, alongside projections of kids playing. Backing it all up is gentle music, as if from a French movie. Having worked in video since the 1980s, Peili specializes in showing repetitive actions and images that somehow can't help creating suspense.

One of the original artists showing with Tilton is Leo Kopers, a Belgian whose most unforgettable work is a mechanized sculpture that looks like a table draped with a white tablecloth. When a motor is turned on, the work spins to become a whirling dervish.

Artists are not constrained here. You never know what you're going to see, and it's possible the gallery doesn't, either, until the time of the show.

Ubu

16 East 78th Street,

between Madison and Fifth Avenues

(212) 794-4444

Tuesday through Saturday,

11 A.M. to 6 P.M.

Ubu has the most consistently imaginative invitations to its exhibition openings—a pink doll's leg mounted on an announcement, for example—and shows to go with them. The gallery reverberates with high-spirited mischievousness and a sense of intellectual and social adventure. Its mission is to expose the roots and branches of the century's various avant-garde movements, underscoring the notion "nothing new under the sun." And if you don't get it, whatever "it" is, owners Rosa Esman, Jack Banning, and Adam Boxer—gregarious all—will eagerly help you.

Among the most influential works you'll find here that continue to seem shocking and fresh are the photographs, installations, and drawings of the Germany-based Hans Bellmer (1902–75). Focusing on the erotic side of Surrealism and gender confusion, Bellmer's images present disturbing concoctions of women and dolls in all manner of disarray, with a special emphasis on their sexual attributes. With his subjects tied up and tangled, Bellmer prefigured the likes of Cindy Sherman while addressing many contemporary issues.

The Russian Constructivists are also often in evidence, with their seminal typographic and geometric works. Their influence can't be avoided in the works of Pop artists

Jasper Johns and Robert Rauschenberg, in those of Conceptualists like Barbara Kruger, Jenny Holzer, and Lawrence Weiner, and on billboards everywhere. Celebrating technology, progress, and new materials, artists like Alexander Rodchenko and Laszlo Moholy-Nagy, who are shown here, tried through a strict formalism to strip art of emotion and embellishment—in essence rebelling against the excesses of the past.

TWENTIETH-CENTURY ART AND PHOTOGRAPHY; 20S AND 30S DADA, SURREALISM, CONSTRUCTIVISM, FLUXUS, POP, AND CONTEMPORARY ART

Speaking for the present is the politico-feminist-Pop-Conceptualist Yoko Ono, whose Surrealist-derived installations reveal her non–John Lennon–connected talents. And, always of the moment are the small drawings, paintings, and prints of that man-of-all-styles Sol LeWitt, one of the few artists today who can get away with making gorgeous works that critics don't dismiss as being too "decorative."

The spirit of the past in the present that prevails at Ubu is very welcome at this moment, when it's easy to believe that the avant-garde is really new. It rarely is.

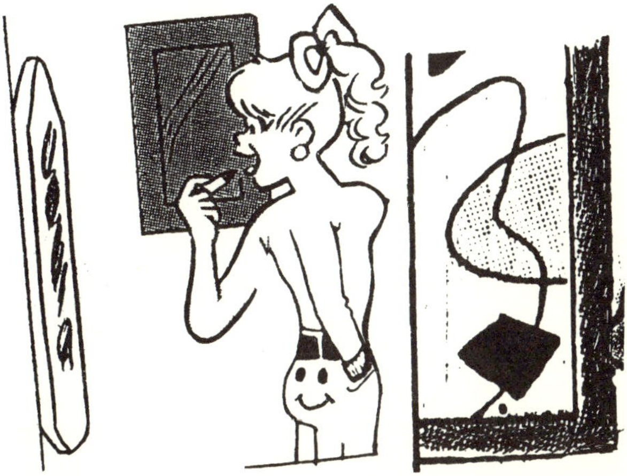

MICHAEL WERNER

21 EAST 67TH STREET, 3RD FLOOR,

BETWEEN MADISON AND FIFTH AVENUES

(212) 988-1623

MONDAY THROUGH SATURDAY,

10 A.M. TO 6 P.M.

Michael Werner, a floor-through gallery in a dignified town house, has an old-fashioned elegance and almost haughty reserve. Ring the buzzer, step into the discreet anteroom, and ascend in the elevator. This is uptown—quiet, less assuming than the converted warehouses and factories of Chelsea and SoHo. The art, too, tends to be smaller and more intimate, and often highbrow with a sense of history.

The gallery specializes in German artists. It shows many works on paper, paintings, and tabletop sculptures. It also sometimes presents installations, like Sigmar Polke's pans of potatoes, echoing the potato-head theme that runs through his works, and the late American conceptual artist James Lee Byars's roomful of mirrored vitrines, suggesting infinite regression and repetition.

Owner Michael Werner started out with—and still has—a gallery in Cologne. He came to New York to codirect a gallery with the headline-stealing gallery owner Mary Boone, called the Mary Boone/Michael Werner Gallery. The alliance broke up, and his own uptown gallery went on to specialize in what Werner knows best—20th-century German art, particularly figurative works by Joseph Beuys, Markus Lüpertz, Georg Baselitz, Jörg

Immendorf, and Polke. But he also shows some of the lush, nature-tinged abstract paintings of the Danish artist Per Kirkeby.

MODERN AND CONTEMPORARY EUROPEAN AND AMERICAN ART, PARTICULARLY BY GERMAN ARTISTS

This is a serene place to view what can sometimes be strong, disturbing art. Beuys's sculpture, for example, suggesting death and bondage, comes off all the more powerfully when set against the warm wood floors and bathed in the soft, diffused light of the gallery's main space. The tendency toward expressionistic art, like that of Lüpertz, Baselitz, and Immendorf, also takes on a more dramatic tension when viewed in these surroundings.

Werner commented once in an interview, "Though I'm not a good dealer, I manage to get along because the others are half asleep." Such a remark is indicative of his gallery's subtly provocative nature, its independence, and its lack of concern for the fashions and opinions of the moment.

ZABRISKIE

41 EAST 57TH STREET, 4TH FLOOR,
CORNER OF MADISON AVENUE
(212) 752-1223
TUESDAY THROUGH SATURDAY,
10 A.M. TO 5:30 P.M.

Virginia Zabriskie has been in business since 1955 and during that period has presented some of the most interesting avant-garde work of the not-so-distant past and of the more established present. The trajectory runs from Man Ray—the Dadaist and Surrealist, who like Conceptualists today dabbled in many genres, most notably photography, and aimed to shock—to the contemporary photographer Nicholas Nixon, who makes intimate portraits of his family.

Sometimes, however, the gallery does things on a larger scale, as when it installed "The Hansa Gallery (1952–59) Revisited," a show that included such diverse artists as Allan Kaprow, an originator of the Happening (he coined the term in 1959), closely related to Performance art; the abstract-landscape painter Wolf Kahn; and the junk-material sculptor Richard Stankiewicz. In

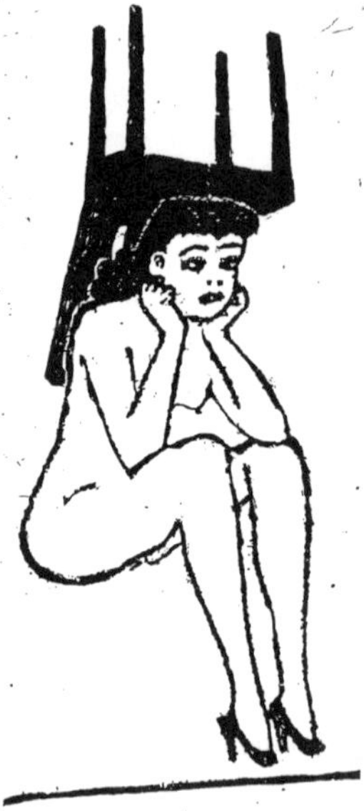

one funkily furnished room, visitors were invited to make breakfast for themselves.

Modern and contemporary American and European art; vintage and contemporary photography

Stankiewicz made his mark with abstract constructions that often resembled figures and animals. That was mostly in the 1950s and '60s. Recently Zabriskie showed him in another light, focusing on his less-famous, more Abstract Expressionist drawings in black India ink poured and brushed on paper, which connect his entire oeuvre.

Dada, Fluxus, Surrealism, and a touch of every avant-garde movement in the United States and abroad appear at Zabriskie. The French photographer Claude Cahun, who had a large retrospective at the gallery, mysteriously disappeared during the Second World War. She was an early cross-dresser who photographed herself in many costumes, playing with questions of gender and identity, prefiguring such artists today as, Cindy Sherman.

One formative avant-gardist featured at Zabriskie is the Swiss Neo-Realist Daniel Spoerri, who gives us a slice of his life by declaring his everyday environments to be art. One way he does this is by applying resin to a table covered with food, cigarette butts, and dirty dishes, and then hanging the "work" on a wall, preserving it forever.

The French artist Ben Vautier (sometimes simply Ben), shares his deadpan sensibility with installations of his environment, including entire re-created rooms. But he also makes environments simply by writing on walls—mostly his name in black in a pleasingly rounded script. Zabriskie provides a clean, well-lighted place for reflecting quietly on modernity then and now.

David Zwirner

43 Greene Street,
between Broome and Grand streets
(212) 966-9074
Tuesday through Saturday,
10 A.M. to 6 P.M.

David Zwirner aims for the cutting edge but generally at the high end. This six-year-old gallery features international artists working in media ranging from the ordinary to the simply weird. Paintings here by Toba Khedoori are deceptively simple and effectively enigmatic. Black line drawings of a bus, perhaps, or segments of apartment buildings on very large sheets of fragile white or neutral paper convey for some viewers uncomfortable feelings of disorientation, melancholy, or abandonment.

Installations by her sister, Rachel Khedoori, involve film projections and sculptural installations. A model of a room, for instance, which visitors can enter and sit in, is accompanied by film images and mirrors. The outdoor shots of boats on the water, of a street of houses projected inside the room, blend interior and exterior, and point to the subjectivity of perception and the elusiveness of a sense of place.

The Belgian painter Luc Tuymans also creates unease, in beautiful, seductive paintings in soft pastel tones of faces and ordinary household objects. Images that are at first elusive seem to develop under our scrutiny, like photographic negatives, to reveal biting satire and poisonous, threatening scenarios. Consider a cheerful container of household cleanser, for example, that is actually highly toxic. It takes just a moment.

Franz West, a sculptor who shows here regularly, also specializes in viewing the familiar, making objects bafflingly endearing, hideously repellent, or simply unrecognizable—a new breed of object that poses on a pedestal without any distinguishing features. Two plaster chairs, for instance, face each other, with a big white cube hanging between them and a sign advising that you can sit on the chairs but should not touch the cube.

Other times artist Jason Rhoades spreads and then spreads some more of his various garage-sale-type wares all over the gallery creating strange, malfunctioning machinery that operates to no purpose. Sometimes it's just a pile of stuff. Rhoades makes a "natural" kind of architecture that we can all aspire to; we just may not want to. As they say today, "Whatever."

The video artist Stan Douglas examines the way we perceive what we see on television and in films. He often manipulates scenes from famous movies, changing their speed, synchronization, or simply taking scenes out of context and playing them repeatedly, thereby intensfying their meanings. Also working with video, Diana Thater sometimes creates rooms and environments simply out of video projections (so it doesn't matter where you actually are.) This gallery is bold, and even if its offerings are not always to your taste, it does possess a sophisticated kind of international moxie.

Index by Neighborhood

Chelsea

Midtown

SoHo

Upper East Side

A

B

C

D

E

F

G

L

M

N

O

P

T

U

V

W

Y

Z

About the Author

Barbara Stone is an editor and writer. She regularly makes the rounds of New York's art galleries and believes that however serious art is, it can also be fun.

About the Artist

Steve Gianakos lives and works in New York and Chania, Crete. He likes good food and girls.

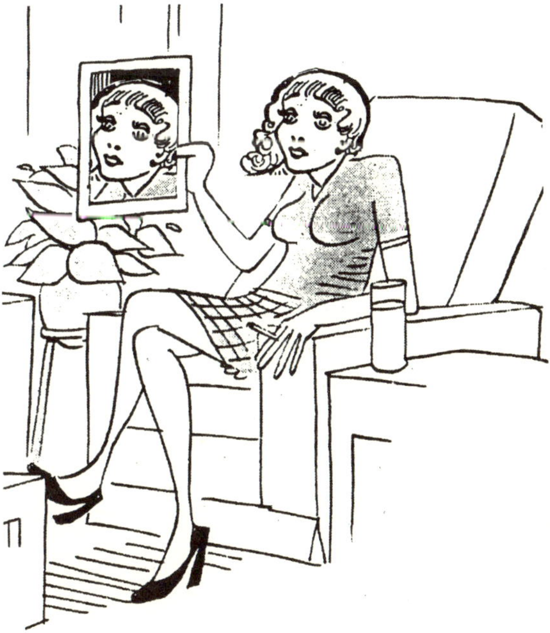